THE PARIAH'S SYNTAX
NOTES FROM AN INNOCENT MAN

Byron Case

redbat books
2013

Printed in the United States of America

First Trade Paperback Edition: September 2013

ISBN 978-0-9895924-0-6
Library of Congress Control Number: 2013947651

Published by
redbat books
2901 Gekeler Lane
La Grande, OR 97850
www.redbatbooks.com

Text set in Adobe Jenson Pro and Rockwell Bold.

Book design by Kristin Summers, redbat design | www.redbatdesign.com

CONTENTS

The Pariah's Syntax

INTRODUCTION

In the beginning was the word. Well, *words*, actually.

I started writing even before I could tie my own shoes—little stories, to begin with, as though testing my stride, of the kind many kids make up and bind, using a hole-punch and yarn, between garish construction-paper covers. On occasion I transformed these stories into comic strips, drawn with a draftsmanlike attention to detail, which were in no way funny. Usually they didn't try to be. The focus of my stories were characters who were very different and therefore misunderstood, ostracized, or hunted for being exceptional.

One character who showed up in a whole series of ill-fated tales, when I was seven-ish, was Dr. Droid, a humanoid alien, three feet tall, with stark-white Albert Einstein hair, whose spacecraft crashed on Earth during a biological and anthropological study mission, stranding him trillions of light years from home, with the ship's onboard artificial intelligence as his only companion. The doctor became a comic strip because I thought that illustrating his awful physique made for a more striking juxtaposition with his nature than words alone could. (I was *that* kind of kid.) Horrendously mutilated by the crash-landing, the doctor was "repaired" by his ship's AI, which grafted scavenged robot parts to him, including a wired interface port to substitute for his ruined voice box, and a set of inept claw hands that made it impossible for him to perform the delicate sample-gathering required by the mission he'd been passionate about completing. Mute and crippled, he hid in the forest, in what remained of his ship. The real drama came when he sneaked into civilization for provisions. He was ultimately spotted, of course. Terrified rural townspeople first ran him into the woods, then local law enforcement reconnoitered his crash site, after which the Army and Air Force, misconstruing the doctor's motives as hostile, visited upon him a horrific, fiery demise.

The thing was, Dr. Droid was a benevolent, sympathetic character—several times in the strip, he rescued animals that were being hunted—not the Frankenstein's monster the human characters presumed him to be. A psychiatrist might've had something to say about a young child authoring such a story.

My parents, always willing to aid and abet my precocity, gave me an old manual Remington typewriter around that time—a hulking black thing with a velour-lined case I could barely lug around the house—and that changed everything. Suddenly I could press a key way, deep down into the machine's steely innards and have the corresponding letter imprint to a page, thereby saving me the excruciating hours of pen work previously required whenever I perched my waifish form at our dining-room table to create worlds. I got to be a decent typist, despite the typewriter being so unaccommodating to little fingers.

When they were complete, I took my stories next door to share with the elderly housebound neighbor lady, who nodded gravely as I recited each sentence with didactic precision. An introverted boy who preferred quiet contemplation to the raucous games of my peers, I made more social calls to the old woman's house than to all the noisy, Kool-Aid-and-Twinkie-fueled neighborhood kids' places, by far. To the old lady, I was a special, brilliant boy; to other kids, I was just a freak. Why *wouldn't* I prefer to share my stories with a receptive audience?

Writing remained an important, if not vital part of my life as I grew. I was probably the only ten-year-old in town to assiduously chronicle my thoughts in a hardcover journal. At fifteen I cofounded and edited an underground newsletter for a friend's high school. The newsletter was banned by school authorities, improbably, upon the release of its second issue, which took an anti-bullying, pro-diversity theme. The following year, I took an internship at my hometown paper, the *Kansas City Star*, where Ernest Hemingway had also written, many decades prior, and where my writing was published widely for the very first time. I wrote poetry throughout my teens, which was actually, at times, not terrible. I blogged on my personal website before the word *blog* existed. Entering my twenties, I hammered out a weekly column for a dotcom-bubble-era online humor magazine. Yet, for all this, I never once thought of myself as a writer.

I can be slow to notice things.

Repeatedly exploring the theme of ostracism in my childhood stories had been prophetic, in a way. I had a growing sense, early on, of being quite different. Of course, everyone's different—some are just more different than most. I was socially retarded, literal-minded, bad at small talk and unaware of other's boundaries. My movements and attitude were equally rigid, and I was as outspoken as I was arrogant—a noxious combination. I stuck to the margins, making few friends. What social attachments I did manage to forge were with listless college-aged depressives, like myself. Some were deeply troubled—suicidal, and worse. In the same way I was blind to the obvious in myself, I couldn't see how seriously some of my friends needed help, and this ignorance led to much exposure to youthful tragedy. One of these tragedies led, belatedly, to a shock: midway through my twenty-second year, I was arrested and charged with my friend Anastasia's three-year-unsolved murder.

The journal I kept in jail, awaiting the fiasco of a trial that would follow, was my way of weathering the storm of confusion and fear roiling inside my usually placid brain. It seemed the right thing to do, recording for posterity my Kafkaesque journey through the legal system, which I believed *had* to end with prosecutors dropping the case, or with a jury acknowledging my innocence. *When this is over*, I decided, *I'm going to write a book.* I wanted to lay bare the ease with which my accuser, an ex-girlfriend, manipulated the system purely out of spite, and to use my story as a cautionary tale about the danger of getting involved with troubled people, no matter how good your intentions nor how strong your desire to fix them.

I was found guilty of armed criminal action and first-degree murder. My respective sentences, run concurrently, were for life and life without the possibility of parole. This meant that, without a court overturning the verdict, or without a governor's pardon, I was to spend the rest of my days locked in a concrete box; mine was a slow death sentence.

Coming to prison felt like the ultimate rejection by society, a final voting off the island, an unambiguous "You're different, and we don't want you around." My frustration at this, my sadness and anger, needed to be directed *somewhere*, so I committed it all to paper. There were no computers to use, so I bought an electronic typewriter, plastic and loud, from the prison's canteen. I bought it before even considering purchasing a television, and used it for hours and hours every day. Some of what I wrote on it I shared with friends, in letters. Like a drowning man reaching for whatever he can grasp, to keep from going under, I maintained a frenzied *rat-a-tat* correspondence. When replies came, they were full of praise for the essayistic tales I shared of prison life, and for my moving meditations on the past.

More than a few times, friends encouraged me to write a book; however, I no longer felt as though I had a book in me. Kind words about my writing, by those I loved, were ample. Moreover, I had come to loathe the idea of writing for strangers, which is what writing a book is really about. Strangers, people like the jury I believed had been too stupid to see the truth, didn't deserve my hard-wrought words.

This misanthropy only got worse with time. Being thrown into the hermetic society of prison, I was as much an outcast as ever. Sometimes my alien status was comforting, as in the countless instances when I heard from another inmate, "You just don't seem like the type of person who belongs here." More often, such as when my reserved demeanor and preference for solitude got me in trouble (with institutional staff and predacious prisoners alike), my differences were things I wished I could cut from my body, like a disfiguring growth. But I was stuck with being atypical. With stronger feelings of slightedness than I had known before, I turned inward, to writing, more fervently than ever.

It was a cellmate who changed my thinking. A creative, kind, intelligent soul with whom I had the uncanny good fortune to be locked in, in the normally claustrophobic nine-by-eleven floor plan, Jamie was someone I'd have befriended even if the social pickings weren't penitentiary-slim. He earned parole within a year of being moved in with me, but our friendship endured. Long after his release, once his free-world life was stable enough that he could turn his thoughts to helping someone other than himself, Jamie offered to transcribe and post some of my writing online, to a social networking site. He knew the case against me was a gross miscarriage;

he wanted to help get the word—and me—out. By stringing together lines and paragraphs, I was already doing the hard part. What he suggested was merely that I continue writing, that he'd handle the particulars of making my output accessible to the world. Seeing no legitimate reason to refuse, outside of antisocial bias, I gave my friend and former cellmate a reluctant go-ahead.

That was 2007, a watershed year. Opening the floodgates to my inner reservoir, writing for a potentially wide readership proved strangely rewarding. Not much later, I was tempted into submitting a piece of fiction to a small-circulation magazine, and to send a few poems out to literary journals. They were published. I wrote more and more, emboldened by acceptances, and, within two years, sold a short memoir piece to what became a best-selling anthology. In little time at all, then, I came to feel less like Dr. Droid, freakish and mute, and more that I was part of a society—literary society. I came to feel like a writer.

As my publication credits grew in number, appeals to various courts came and went. I didn't go anywhere, but the blog that Jamie had started moved to its own domain, pariahblog.com, with an archive of posts that expanded, slowly yet steadily, a few times each month. Six years' writing amounts to a fair bit, and it occurred to me that, after so long, enough material had been amassed to fill the book I'd abandoned the idea of.

Did I dare merely cherry-pick a bushel of posts from the blog and publish them as a half-assed paperback? Would doing that be worthwhile for myself, as a writer, or for you, as a reader? The short answer was no. Although not quite a memoir, the book would have to be more than simply a clump of random personal essays anyone could seek out on the web—it needed to be curated, judiciously culled from the published as well as the previously unread, fitted together in such a way as to propel a reader along its loose narrative arc, starting with memories of my youth, closing with the truths of my inescapable present. If the book couldn't be that, I would not waste my energy. Call me picky.

The slim volume you now hold represents what I believe is some of my best personal writing from prison. It is also a token of the change in my attitude toward writing in general. No longer am I a miser, hoarding my sheafs of typewritten pages like so many bars of gold, stowed away, as though from grasping by unclean hands. I recognize now that writing is, first and foremost, communication. It demands reception, demands a reader. Writing demands to be shared. And who am I to refuse?

CROSSROADS CORRECTIONAL CENTER, 2012

A LIFE AMPHIBIOUS

My father was born with gills and webbed feet, the son of a mermaid and a merchant marine. The earliest photograph of him I have seen was a grade school portrait, which suggests those features—the gills, at least—atrophied as he got older, for they were nowhere to be seen by then. For the entirety of his life, though, as with any creature born of the sea, my father would remain drawn to water and all things aquatic. At eighteen, he enlisted in the United States Navy, where whatever vestigial toe-webbing remained would have been perceived as an asset. He dove freely into untested waters, canoed down rolling river rapids, fished with nets. He collected seashells and coral. He kept tropical fish. I remember the way he'd whisper to them while sprinkling in their food, inviting them to dinner by invoking their secret names: to him they were not angelfish, gourami, or tetra but Streamer-Tail, Little Bubble-Maker, Prism-Darter. They were his piscine friends, exiles from the same kingdom, and they kept him company in his home on dry land.

Of course he owned vessels—a fifteen-foot aluminum canoe, an inflatable raft, a small sailboat. These were the only way my mother and I could accompany him on his watery communions. Creatures of terra firma is what she and I were—awed by the shadowy ubiquity of water in the world, shaky on deck, barely submersible. My father was our fearless captain, ready to brave the storms and show us landlubbers there was little to fear from the murky depths. When he would change tack to head into a squall, or paddle us towards the rocks, we had to wonder whether he hadn't momentarily forgotten our handicap. But always he brought us through, dampened by the spray, most likely, but quite alive. Being with him in the presence of water meant knowing fervency for life; his enthusiasm was contagious.

We towed the sailboat with us one year, on a family vacation to the Florida Keys, when I was a boy. Our first night at the coast, my mother and I slept in the van. Displaying uncharacteristic childlike eagerness, my father spent the night in a sleeping bag on deck, docked in the marina a few hundred feet away. Mosquitoes, of course, left him unmolested. It was blood they craved, not the clear salinity of what his veins pumped. As the sun rose from the center of the Atlantic, Mum and I stumbled salty-eyed into the morning. We found my father already unmoored, gliding aimlessly around the marina on a steady wind he'd been loath to let pass unavailed. He waved to us. There was no telling how long he'd been out. He had to have woken at least an hour before dawn, in order to have time to erect the mast and secure the rigging. Out on the blue, his sails were brimming, his smile gleamed.

The day was long and humid, and by late afternoon had given way to the slate horizon of an impending storm. Since that morning we'd been skirting the coastline. Because we had no radio, no compass, no map—indeed, no navigational equipment of any sort (what kind of an adventure would it have been, otherwise?)—we dropped anchor off a tiny, sandy island with a sliver of clear beach large enough to pitch our tent and light a cookfire. We ate thin vegetable soup with crackers and nibbled on roasted peanuts. The soup scalded my tongue as I sipped too eagerly from a battered tin cup. When the rain came, at first with uncertainty, we retreated but left the tent flaps open so we could watch the clouds tumble and the far-off waves clash. I fell asleep to the popping of fat drops on the canvas and the thick air of our gradually smoldering fire. I dreamt of wild seas.

In the small hours, the three of us awoke, startled. The tide was coming in. It lapped inches from the front of the tent. Already the remains of the fire had been swallowed; now, ever hungry, the water was reaching for us. Pattering rain kept on as we hurriedly pulled stakes and carried our shelter several feet back, to the tree line. As the beach gradually disappeared, we looked on, unsure if the high ground we'd claimed would be high enough to avoid a late night escape back to our boat. I fell back asleep eventually, as did Mum, but Papa was vigilant. His silhouette at the front of the tent reassured me when I woke again, later, to the sound of his whispered supplications to the waves.

The scene at dawn was much different. By that time the tide had gone out so far that it had stranded the boat, dry and resting pitifully at an angle, on its keel. Seaweed draped the line to the shore, imparting a look of abandonment, like a ghost ship in spite of its cheerful blue hull. Not knowing when the waters would again rise, my father set to work righting her, the way people attend to a beached whale. Now pushing, now rocking, now patting her belly, he coaxed the boat back into her element.

Packed in and hungry, we set course for the mainland beyond our horizon. Arcane sailor knowledge or natant instinct guided my father at the tiller as he steered us toward the marina from which we'd put out. The wind that morning was robust and consistent. I stood aft of the small cabin, catching briny air in my nostrils. In my ears was nothing but that whooshing roar. Then Papa said something indistinct and my mother laughed. I turned, hoping to hear. They were smiling—such wide, open smiles!—and with the sun radiant on his face I watched my father draw a deep, contented breath, and surveyed his neck and jawline for the row of fishy slits I knew just had to be there.

JAMAICA, 1987

My father and I entered the warm water of midafternoon from the beach equipped only with his flippers, goggles and snorkel, and an inflatable pool raft with a slender bit of rope knotted to it. He was still in his thirties, still of average build, and wore the green trunks that were old then, yet would make an appearance, ten years later, on our final canoe trip. My trunks were red and, because I was only seven—too young for real adventure stories—devoid of such provenance. Both of us, as well as my mother, bore the darkened skin and sun-bleached hair of Yankees gradually succumbing to the siren song of the Caribbean: glorious scenery, welcoming people, the casual ethos, the culinary pleasures. I still get cravings for authentic jerk pork and an icy bottle of Ting.

Our mission that particular day was primal hunter-gatherer stuff. We would swim out in search of conchs to gather up, return to the beach, beat them from their shells in an exhausting and somewhat foolish-looking procedure involving tossing the shells against the sand over and over again, then present them to a local woman whose restaurant turned them into a hearty, mouthwatering stew. The stew we'd pay for in extra conchs.

The family spent that month in Negril, in a tent, surrounded by a small grove of thin trees at the edge of the beach. The sand, perhaps, had worked its way under our skin as we slept, or too much ocean air had filled our lungs and veins with a yearning to remain—to leave responsibilities and become a family of expat beach bums, browning and crinkling into human handbags.

My parents had gone so far as to ask about schools. Outside of the cities, everywhere you turned was lush and beautifully saturated with color, and the ocean was never more than a few miles away, wide and blue and welcoming. Some may find it unfathomable, but to go and not be so moved would have been the unthinkable thing.

We waded out until the water was deep enough to swim—my father pulling the raft by its rope, and me alternately swimming alongside him and hanging from its edge. After a time, the sandy floor disappeared completely beneath us, rendering the water a mysterious shade of teal. My father swam on. Teal eventually transitioned into darkness, and this was where he chose to stop. It seemed like hours he'd been pulling. Looking back at the island, my field of vision encompassed a wide swath of glistening shoreline; in front of me lay nothing but the undisturbed sea and a horizon of vivid blues. My father pulled himself partially onto the raft. His large mustache drooped with wetness. He looked something like a walrus.

Taking in the surroundings above water, he said, simply, "This is good."

We waited.

When he'd sufficiently regained his strength, he again donned the goggles and, taking with him nothing more than two lungfuls of air, plopped out of sight with the briefest of splashes. Adrift in the Caribbean, my father beyond reach or sight, I should have been frightened. The serenity of the waning sunlight on calm waters, however, was pervasive, and I was too much in awe of my father's aquatic prowess. How he searched at those depths, without light or fear of barracuda (and for so long!), I did not know or think to ask, but each time, without fail, up he would rise with a conch in each hand. Then, several breaths taken, bearings gathered, he would dive again, often without a word of warning, leaving me to mind those large shells and ensure the gentle sway and flex of the raft didn't cause them to tumble away.

As I sat there, corralling those great, horned seashells with my matchstick legs, I looked out to the open sea, at its bold immensity, and contemplated the distance between us and home. It seemed vast—worlds away from our campsite, the friends I'd made, the frigid waterfalls, the misty mountains. How could I return to Kansas City after all this? Certainly, I'd visited Jamaica before—twice—but in that instant on the open water it all seemed different. I was older; experiences like this held more meaning for me.

Literally then, out of the blue popped my father with three more conchs.

"How many does that give us?" he asked, spitting saltwater away from his lips and breathing deeply.

I counted. "Eleven."

"All right, Kiddo," my father beamed, white teeth, no tusks, but still so lovably walrus-y. "Looks like we've got dinner."

And I forgot all about leaving.

OZ

Awakened by a treeful of excited, laughing kookaburras shortly after sunup, I donned my burgundy robe and tottered down the hall like a crotchety octogenarian. Eleven years old, I already felt world-weary enough to greet the day sourly. The birds' incessant cackles, like some deranged sitcom audience, were mercifully muffled in the kitchen at the back of our rented house, in the suburb of Picnic Point, New South Wales, Australia. Relieved by the quiet, I set to preparing my breakfast.

I always made myself the same thing: a couple of buttered, honey-drizzled crumpets; a bowl of Wheatabix with banana slices; a tall glass of chocolatey, malty Milo. This meal's novelty never wore thin. I treated it as an essential element of my cultural assimilation, as necessary as learning the old traditionals, such as "Botany Bay" and "Waltzing Matilda"; as necessary as educating myself in national trivia, such as the routes of Captain Cook or the developmental stages of the gray kangaroo— a crucially important matter, practically life-or-death.

My parents were recently divorced. My mother, consummate globetrotter and all-round adventuress, decided to begin her life afresh. In later years, Mum's response to the question of how, of the myriad places she might have chosen to move, the Land Down Under won out, amounted to "It seemed like a good idea at the time." This goes a long way toward summarizing her impetuous thinking. It's basically the same reply I got when I asked how the free spirit from Würzburg, Germany, ended up married, with a son, in Kansas City, Missouri, USA: that's just how the dice fell.

As for me, when the divorce was filed I was offered the choice of staying with my father, in the house I'd called home all my life, or of jetting off with Mum to terra incognita. No little boy I could imagine would have chosen differently.

My mother was somehow unfazed by the kookaburras' racket, yet she woke to my stirring. We met at the dining room table, smiling sleepily.

Her day began with a cup of herbal tea and some Vegemite on toast—a contemptible black smear of half-rotten vegetable matter on an otherwise perfectly edible piece of bread. The Vegemite was her own, more daring, adult version of getting Aussie-savvy. She would always insist the spread was actually tasty. Having my assertion of its nastiness validated by many native Australians who wouldn't touch the stuff, our stalemate endured.

My smile sank into a grimace at the sight of the Vegemite. A noise escaped my lips.

Mock-defensively, Mum said, "Not 'Eew,' Byron. You mean to say, 'Yum!'"

She took a bite and stuck a blackened tongue out at me, then slid the plate of toast and salty compost-spread across the table to me. I recoiled, horrified but giggling, and said, "Not in a million years."

After breakfast, we packed wordlessly for our day trip into Sydney. A bag with bottled water and snacks to share.

A book. Mum's Walkman and cassette tapes. My sheet music stand and violin—our reason for spending afternoons, virtually every single Saturday, in the city. These things we toted the four or five kilometers to Revesby, site of the nearest train station. From that small open-air platform, the New South Wales rail system delivered us in short order to Sydney Harbor.

The brief walk from the station to the waterfront took us past a heckling French juggler, across the path of a covey of camera-crazed Asian oglers, and around a moon-faced Aborigine man's shopfront, which spilled out, impeding sidewalk traffic with T-shirt displays and decorative, hand-carved boomerangs. On the quay, by the famous Opera House, were droves of buskers to circumnavigate. Some of the regular fixtures were musicians, like me. Others had mime routines, stand-up comedy acts, or elaborate marionette shows. But the old violinist, always able to claim the same shady spot, no matter the weather or the crowds, was the busker who captured my attention.

His worn, brown suit and battered rancher's hat could have been ten years old as easily as a hundred. The man himself was gaunt and withered, drab, as though under the dust of years. The instrument he played was solid, bearing a patina I knew was unattainable except by many decades of play, and it had a resonance, a caramel-rich depth of sound, that to me epitomized a violin's melancholic air.

Every morning I arrived at the Harbor, there he was; every time I left, the same. His stamina was machinelike; however, no automated device could match the emotion that the old busker drew from his four strings. Invariably I stopped to listen, to absorb what knowledge I could.

This day, after Mum and I had stood by him awhile, he stopped in the middle of a piece, for whatever reason, to aim his bow at the case in my hand and ask, "What d'ya know?"

At odds with his music, his voice was surprising in its coarseness; his accent, distinctly native. Not the best conversationalist anyway, I was too startled to answer him.

"Hmm. Well, d'ya know this?" He leaned into a soaring arpeggio I didn't recognize, a melody like a romping dog overjoyed to be out of its kennel, free. Presently, the man changed his tune. The transition was as jarring as bumping the needle on a turntable: an abrupt gypsy funeral, a low, swooning lament. "What about this one, then?"

I shook my head, uncertain of whether I was expected to be focused on his smooth bow-work, his papery fingers rocking across strings, or his ragged brown shoes.

"Ah well," he grunted. "Yer young yet." And at that, with a wink, he went back to his sheet music, releasing me to claim a spot for myself.

The comparative ineptness of my own form weighed heavily on me as I set up next to a lamp post by the water's edge. Silent gusts of sea air breathed down my shirt collar. I rosined my bow, tuned strings, then took a nervous lungful of air. A clutch of tourists was headed toward me. At the sight of them, I tried to put out of my head all comparisons between my half-size violin and the old man's. I was there, after all, to play, not to think.

Instinct took over. I forsook my usual classical fare and launched into a lively rendition of "Waltzing Matilda." Sure enough, the first coins of the day came falling into the hollow of my open case: *pop-pop-clink!* I beamed at Mum, on the bench across the walk. Her headphones were on and she was reading her novel, but she noticed me and smiled encouragingly back.

I played on, as the day progressed, pausing only long enough to take a sip of water or offload excess coins into a pocket of Mum's bag when my case got too full. Money came steadily. My audiences were tourists and locals alike, and I played my best for them all—the men and the women, the elderly and the toddlers, the Westerners and the Easterners. Reaching out, I played to everyone within earshot. Appreciation came with a few moments' pause, perhaps a comical little jig, then the drop of a coin or two before they moved on.

Despite having been born with the mental age of a forty-five-year-old, there were boyish pursuits that interested me. Model train paraphernalia and Lego bricks didn't come cheap. I received no allowance, therefore the money I earned from busking on the quay paid for such extravagances. Sometimes I visualized the specific acquisition I'd be able to buy with the coins I was accruing, and these moments of eagerness would compel me to continue playing even after my fingers began to ache, or they would motivate me to play that allegro *again*—perhaps for the fourth time in a row—for a promising-looking group of pedestrians headed my way.

But by late afternoon my slender fingers were stiffening, only able to take so much. I called it a day.

Before Mum and I made it back to the station, before we stopped for me to treat her to an ice cream, and before that last breath of salty air was out of our lungs, though, we had to pass the old violinist, still playing, now in the orange-tinged shade of waning Pacific light. As ever, I was struck dumb by the passionate ease of his playing. He moved and sounded no less perfect than when we had passed him, late that morning; the hours he'd stood there had no effect on the sublimity of his music.

From my bag, I pulled a few of the more valuable coins I'd earned. I knelt and set them in his brown-and-red case with careful reverence, a tithe. He didn't stop to acknowledge me as before; though, I didn't really want him to. His smile was small but unmistakable. And even though it was money that lured me, this and the music were why I was there.

I didn't realize then, wrapped up in myself to the point of myopia, like most children, but the old man was almost certainly homeless. Many buskers at the Harbor were. Had I been more aware, I might have borne my relative advantages in mind when giving the violinist his due. I like to think I'm wrong about this, that he, in his worn leather coat and battered shoes, performed to share his talent and make some extra cash, as I did, rather than so he could eat.

That day, though, I just took Mum's hand, and the old man's sweet music followed us along the paving stones leading to the train station. His music probably continued long after we were gone.

THE DRONE

It's like a dream.
Through honeydrunk eyes and wax walls of time,
My first remembered penetrator lies
Dying on backyard grass greener than any
I will ever know, a curling yellowblack
Almost-corpse amid the dandelions, libidinous, pulsing
In his little death ecstatic
(Or agonized) in throes.
The way all insects go takes
Practice to tell, but is
Gorgeous all the same.
And safe shoes, as Mother Nature would herself
Profess, are best. I've not been unshod since.

ONE-MAN ORCHESTRA

Ridiculous in ruin, tragic as
All great art, I sought

My youthful voice through misery, through
Mouths opened I did not have
Before. And how they sang!
From hopelessness dribbled,

Down the notation of these
Sloppy pale blue scales, a rhapsody
            Propelled
By the percussion of my poor, disconsolate
Heart, above which could be heard

        The gasping of an audience.

        A window, politely closing.

A rasping beak on stone.
Then off: swooning
Strings in the air, gentle
And somber.

Finally a timpani, in the basin plinking
—A lullaby.

ALONE IN THE DARK

I was in seventh grade when I started excising all color from my wardrobe. The benefits of wearing black were twofold: first, it somewhat slimmed the pudgy, beanlike physique I attained in my tween years; second, it eliminated the challenge of selecting ensembles of complementary shades and patterns from my closet each morning. When my father took me shopping, I chose clothes that seemed identical to what my peers were wearing, yet my schoolmates saw right through my efforts at fitting in, as if I were a huge beetle in acidwashed jeans. My hopeless fashion sense had been fuel for the fires of mockery that blazed around me in the school hallways. "Hey, Einstein, who dressed you this morning—the circus?" and "Nice shirt you got there, Brainiac!" flicked at my heels as I marched from class to class.

Being an awful dresser had less to do with my lack of middle-school friends than being abnormally smart and socially inept. I spoke precisely, almost academically, in the default conversational style of Monologue, fumbling my way through back-and-forth exchanges and rarely acknowledging others' level of interest in the topic at hand. To use a term from our socially networked era, I was *unfriendable*. After suffering on the pyre of ridicule for so long, the growing prevalence of black clothing in my closet became symbolic, representative of the charred remains of my hopes for peer acceptance.

Leaving home on any given day, wearing a personal uniform of monochromatic dress shirt and slacks, nearly identical to what I wore the day before, the day before that, and the day before that, my reputation began to shift. I went from being considered freakishly intelligent to merely freakish. Those hateful schoolmates were right to think mine was a morose presence; my bookishness made me pale and solitary, and I was largely expressionless—impassive as a statue, even when bullies shoved me in the halls. Tormentors, always straining to get a rise, wanted to know where the funeral was. ("What funeral?" I was naive enough to ask.) Then came the recurring question of whether I slept in a coffin. Oh, if only those twelve- and thirteen-year-olds could have seen me a couple of years later, after I embraced my pariah status and began hurling my differences into people's faces.

I knew how people often reacted to the sight of me at sixteen, with my black hair and nails, spiked leather dog collars, and multiple piercings—it was tough not to notice. When elderly women stared at me in the grocery store, when the guy I sat next to at the diner counter moved a few stools down with his plate, or when the gangstas huddled outside the gas station saw me coming and uttered a collective, awed "What the fuck?" my soul cracked a little smile. That the manner in which I dressed profoundly disturbed those people's perceptions of the world was something I relished, even without fully understanding it. That they incorrectly assumed all sorts of things about my lifestyle and morality was something I couldn't have cared less about. The androgynous, postapocalyptic-funeral aesthetic was my litmus test: if you didn't make a big deal of how I looked, you might be a decent human being—a philosophy cribbed from Bernard Baruch, who wrote, "Those who mind don't matter, and those who matter don't mind."

This was, of course, an imperfect system. There were some who saw the pale pretty-boy as a lonely waif to be taken advantage of. I had to learn the hard way that just because someone accepted me didn't mean he or she was good. Plenty had ulterior motives. My mind seemed incapable of making the type of generalizations involved in pattern recognition. Many were the times I found myself in a new friend's apartment (often an older, gay man, because they were just *so nice* to me), being served an alcoholic drink or offered illicit drugs, thinking, *the last time someone offered, I had to fend off advances*, without a single warning light illuminating the murkiness of my brain. Once that evening's host proved himself as lusty as those before him, I found myself fleeing yet another set of premises, cursing people's unpredictability.

Superficial identification methods were all I had. At various times, after I came of age, I fell in with subcultures whose standards of personal style were similar to mine. In no time at all, though, I discovered how little I belonged in their company. The goths, with their too-serious attitudes, didn't appreciate how I made a joke of everything as we posted ourselves around the vacant dance club floor, minor-key synth drones and the smoke of clove cigarettes threatening claustrophobia. The self-declared vampires were too theatrical, too *woo-woo* to get along with, the few times I deigned to show up at the old Masonic lodge where they were known to cluster like dust in the corners, immersed in some ridiculous game of Let's Pretend. And as for the fetish clubbers, they were a disappointment: only weird in public one night a week—and even then, purely for sexual reasons—before trading their leather and latex for sensible skirts and suits at dawn. For their part, each of these groups agreed that I was an awkward fit. Hardly a wonder—our brains didn't even work the same.

It was weeks after I turned thirty that I finally learned how my brain had everything to do with my perennial outsider status.

I was born with a high-functioning form of the autistic spectrum disorder known as Asperger's syndrome. AS is a neurological condition generally marked by a person's pervasive social deficiencies, literal-mindedness, difficulty processing certain sensory input, and hindered emotional expression. Those of us who have AS often have above-average intelligence and a narrow (but very, very deep) set of personal interests. We also lack the concept known as Theory of Mind—the ability to discern what others may be thinking, and to realize that, whatever it is, it's probably quite different from our own thoughts. Knowing how the things I do will be received can be difficult. Ditto for things I say.

Friends have jokingly accused me of coming from K-PAX (after the Kevin Spacey movie of that name, in which his character believes himself an alien), and of being a pod person, hatched from a cocoon. Is it any wonder why AS is known as "wrong planet syndrome" among witty Aspergians?

The interim between those fraught middle-school days in the early '90s and my 2008 revelation was confusing and often painful. Incapable of comprehending others' behaviors or some of the most basic social cues left me the victim of my own ineptness. Frequent faux pas made me few friends and several enemies. I was often lonely and, even after dropping out of the social meat grinder that was high school, regularly beset by rumors. Later came a suicide attempt, cocaine addiction, an arrest for stealing, an abusive and codependent relationship, and more tragedy than you'd care to read about here.

Making sense of people is a lifelong series of trial-and-error tests. Finding a niche in which to fit took more than half my lifetime. And I'm still working at it.

The whole human race is one big anthropology study to me. My research is all-consuming. Since I was a teenager, I have read books on subjects ranging from psychology to philosophy, from cold-reading techniques to marketing strategies—anything that might give me a better idea of how to function alongside neurotypical brains. Through this diligence, I have developed an action-reaction mental flowchart for interfacing with my fellow humans, and am perpetually making changes to it—tweaking, honing, perfecting. Many still regard me as a freak, a weirdo, or worse, but at least I have a clue of how to properly interact in social settings these days. I'm also a much better judge of character.

My personal style continues to skew heavily to the Dark Side. My many friends, unconventional in their own, quieter ways, are wearers of color, and none have audacious style (unless you count deliberately mismatched socks or the smiling face of actress Betty White on earrings). To look at us in our natural habitats, you might never suspect we share enough common ground to be the devoted friends we are. Oh, but we are.

It's funny: it took me almost twenty years to figure out that clothes don't necessarily define the wearer, which was exactly the lesson I spent my persecuted youth wishing everyone else would hurry up and learn.

WINTER WONDERLAND

The 1996 ice storm took out power across Kansas City for days. Not only were lines and transformers down, an inch-thick armor of frozen water toppled whole trees, which barricaded suburban streets with their dendrite forms. Roads were encased for blocks on end. For many, escape from their homes by car was impossible. Not that most risked road travel, given the conditions. Public Works trucks canvassed nonstop with salt and sand, but fighting the storm's effects proved a Sisyphean task. In their desperation, gas and electric companies had to enlist out-of-state assistance to do triage on the extensive damage. For thousands, life came to a standstill.

Warmth drained quicker than expected from the suburban three-bedroom my roommate and I—both seventeen; both precociously independent—shared. As the last sunlit hour slipped away, there was no indication we would have heat restored that night. Houses on the next block still had power, though, and this observation led us to believe a hot deep-dish might await intrepid souls hardy enough to make the half-mile journey east, to Torre's Pizza. Neither my roommate nor I wanted to sit around eating a cold dinner on such a night, candlelit or otherwise.

We slid into layers of sweaters and coats, and extinguished the near-bonfire of illumination by which we'd been reading in the living room. As Aaron, my roommate, crowned himself with his brown old-man hat, he joked, "Just so you know, if it starts to look like we won't make it, I'm hungry enough not to have qualms about resorting to cannibalism."

"That's no good," I said, covering my grimace with a scarf. "I'm hardly a meaty Brazilian soccer player."

"With all that time in front of the computer, I'll bet you're like veal."

"My stomach's growling. Let's go before this gets all Donner Party-freaky."

We were sobered by the state of things beyond our door. The spangled surface of everything was blue with the city's faint lambency, and alive with sound—the collective groans of miles of ice-weighted objects being pulled earthward. Had we held perfectly still awhile, the stinging flurry from the sky might have encased us as it had all else. Moving quickly through it as we did was to witness a rare beauty, like traversing the interior of a diamond.

Some parkour got us over and through the labyrinth of creaking branches obstructing the end of our block. After that, it was a more conventional walk down a wider, flatter route to the welcoming yellowed glow of Torre's. It seemed other neighborhood residents had the same idea for dinner; my famished friend and I pushed through the front door, frozen faces first, into a round of cheery hellos and not a few jokes about being fellow survivors of the winter apocalypse. For everyone's dedication to local business, drinks were on the house: iced-down sodas and tea, but still.

The next morning, Aaron and I built a fire pit in the backyard. The wind had stilled in the night, leaving something easily mistakable for warmth as we squinted against the brilliant daylight, toting scrap two-by-fours from the basement. With some newspaper and an old broom—*voilà!*: flames by which to cook. Aaron retrieved chairs off the patio; I raided the quieted refrigerator for perishables. We never ate such a breakfast as that. Omelets full of onions and fire-roasted tomatoes and peppers, fried potatoes in little pools of butter, a half-gallon of milk to wash it down with, and, later, coffee made from billy-boiled water poured oh-so slowly through our coffeemaker's detached basket of grounds. We ate and drank it all outside, in the crackling whiteness, like we were the last men alive. Nothing echoed, every sound an unfamiliar intimacy, the clinking of our forks nearer than I've ever heard, and our food magically better for that isolation.

For lunch we roasted Hebrew National hot dogs and drank mugs of rich cocoa with a flotilla of miniature marshmallows, sitting in our chairs and watching steam almost crystallize as it rose from our beverages and mouths alike. Neither of us spoke. Off in the distance of a neighboring yard was a cardinal, pecking at seeds in a feeder, and we watched him until something unseen and silent startled him away.

Regarding the light switch with a kind of mistrust, on the third day's return of electricity, Aaron said, "There's something to that, reading by candlelight. We should keep it up for awhile—the fire, all of it. Let's just unplug some of this stuff and go on living without the modern conveniences."

His naive enthusiasm was infectious, I'll admit. So we did it. But of course, amid the neighbors' resumption of their usual activity, it couldn't last. Snowblowers tore at the air. Nearby traffic hummed. After sunset, streetlights dug pits in the darkness. The cardinal made his home in some far-off tranquil field that only those with wings could reach.

THE KIDS GIVE *GUTTER BALL*
A WHOLE NEW MEANING

One temperate evening in late spring of my seventeenth year, I sat smoking with my friends Brahm and Tara on Paul's quaint concrete front porch. The house was small, a remnant of an era when that part of the city was still suburbs. Even Paul, oldest among us, couldn't have known a time when traffic noise and sirens did not reach his rented home. Around the city's haze, darkness was creeping into crevasses, and we were idly contemplating a plan of action, in the way of many Midwestern American youth, when I noticed a wheelbarrow on the neighbor's curb—a wheelbarrow full of bowling balls.

The narrow street's residents had set their trash out for morning pickup, but Paul's neighbors obviously expected a bit more than the usual performance out of their sanitation engineers. Nine bowling balls! Of all the things to throw away. And what a way to get them to the street: in a perfectly serviceable garden implement. As with much curbside trash, the juxtaposition was humorous while also being baffling.

Nine bowling balls… *in a wheelbarrow.*

Brahm asked the sanest question. "What garbage man's going to expend the time and effort to lift a bunch of heavy balls into his truck?"

"It's not a bunch," I said. "Bananas come in bunches; bowling balls, plural—that's called a *passel*."

Unsmiling, Tara took a drag from her Camel, flipped her hair and deadpanned, "Oh, yes. Funny."

My humor is of a singular brand, but Brahm was right. No two men, however hale and fit, were going to take away the balls, by either picking them up one at a time or by heave-hoing the entire wheelbarrow. Our pal Paul's neighbors were asking too much.

"Someone could still use these," said Tara upon inspecting the mound. The balls were of all different colors and weights, some in solid colors, some with eccentric swirly patterns. Two were flecked metallic, like Hot Wheels toy cars. Only one appeared damaged, with a big sidelong split in its pearly shell. "I guess they just didn't feel like playing anymore."

"I wouldn't mind a game," I said, looking up and down the street. "Too bad they didn't throw away a set of pins—we could play right here."

Sometimes when you're with friends and someone has a fantastic idea, the way the idea surfaces seems, when reflected upon later, to have been born of the combined consciousness—groupthink. This was the case at that moment, standing under a buzzing yellow streetlight with two of my best friends, when we decided to go street bowling.

A surprisingly large percentage of homeowners are funny about others making off with their trash. Having dumpster-dived and scavenged a good deal in my limited years, I had learned how some people's paranoia could turn innocent salvage operations into scary dressings-down ("Get outta there, you parasites!") or worse. So we asked for, and received, Paul's okay to load the spherical contents of his neighbors' wheelbarrow into the trunk of my busted-up Pontiac and head for the hills.

We figured the best pins available would be empty bottles, and that the best place to turn into our personal alley would be an out-of-the-way stretch of road where some broken glass wouldn't make a whole lot of difference to anyone. Step one was easy and could also technically be considered neighborhood beautification. Anywhere with liquor stores, pawn shops, and mobile phone depots will do for finding a slew of discarded bottles. By picking them up, we'd be doing a public service. Conveniently enough, a sketchy midtown strip wasn't far away.

We drove slowly, in the far-right lane, eyes peeled for cast-off forty-ouncers glinting in the grassy median. Each time we stopped at the curb to retrieve some, my friends leapt out, laughing at the silliness of what we were doing, then dropping another stinky armful into the trunk to acquaint itself with the balls. Reports from the back seat each time were that more bottles had been crushed; we hadn't even thought about keeping the balls from rolling around freely.

"Your trunk is full of glass dust," Tara told me with a smirk.

For fun, and to emphasize how little I cared about the state of my battered wreck's little-used stowage compartment, I gave the steering wheel a slight tug. Behind us was heard a muffled *thunk, ka-thunk!* We all giggled like schoolchildren.

We ended up on Cliff Drive, a twisty-turny route in woodsy northeast Kansas City that, in spite of being officially historical, was pretty shabby. Pull-offs had, in some distant era, offered motorists fine cliffside views of a wealthy part of the city, but were now litter-strewn, overgrown, and under-trafficked—in a word, perfect.

I pulled in at one of these ill-lit roadside crescents, crushed glass from parties of yore crackling beneath my tires. A six-inch retaining wall on the cliffside wouldn't have prevented incautious drivers from rolling right off, free-falling through trees and a dense overgrowth of vines, into a carpeting of litter—empty bottles, plastic cups, cigarette packs, and who-knows-what-all—thirty feet below. The lack of guardrails or wire evidenced the location's bygone relevance. It had been all but abandoned by the city. I cut the engine and popped the trunk, announcing, "Welcome to Cliff Drive Lanes, people!"

Brahm and I agreed to let the lady bowl first. We crouched to set up a triangle of ten bottles away from the road, near the retaining wall, while Tara picked a blue ball from the trunk. She put the road between us and rubbed her hands vigorously, preparing for action. (Some distance from the pins was necessary to approximate actual bowling; we were determined to preserve a *little* authenticity.) As soon as we were clear of the estimated glass shrapnel radius, she let fly. The ball rumbled past Brahm and me like a blur—the girl had a good arm—smashed through seven of our makeshift pins, bounced with a hollow *pok!* off some hitherto unseen ripple in the asphalt, and disappeared into the blackness, without a sound.

"Damn," Tara said. "Did it go over?"

Brahm shot to the edge, his long hair flying, and peered down over the low wall. Whatever he expected to see wasn't there. "Oh yeah," he chortled. "It's gone."

"Should that be a penalty?" I wondered aloud.

"Hey, way to make up rules as you go along," said Tara, genuinely upset. "I should get a pass if we're playing that way."

"No rules, just play," Brahm said. He stooped into my trunk and chose a ball. Tara and I crowded him as we retrieved replacements for the obliterated "pins." When he took a long-legged running start, I knew my mischievous friend intended to send his ball the way Tara's had gone. This was understandable. There's something kind of funny about launching a sixteen-pound composite-plastic piece of sports equipment off a cliff. When only three pins shattered, Brahm didn't mind. He was too preoccupied by the *pok!* that sent his brown orb into oblivion. "That was great," he said.

Not all our balls went over. Our fun wouldn't have lasted very long if they had. Street bowling quickly became a sport of some finesse as we worked to find the sweet spot—that ideal inertia for breaking as many pins as possible without sending the balls down to a wooded grave. Recovering the ones just bowled became an even bigger challenge than bowling itself, because the road's incline often sent them caroming to the right. We laughed to watch whoever was on fetching duty scuttle downhill after a runaway. The posture required was a through-the-legs-backwards catch that stripped the fetcher, hilariously, of any possible dignity. All this was worth the road grime and pulverized glass that clung to our palms.

When the last ball, already cracked almost in two before I bowled it, rolled erratically away from me, completely missing the final remaining pins, and, with a *grrrr, pok!* vanished, the three of us brushed our hands on our clothes.

"Hey, I sparkle," exclaimed Tara, grinning and holding her tiny palms up to the light. We all looked. They glimmered like fairy dust.

NEGLIGENCE PRAYER

So naive this subject and his infinite
Reliance on the hospital's rotating host—
Red-haired, blonde, and steely—in their fluttering,
Fussy buzzing. Forgive him, but he's
Too heartsick to keep watch. He trusts,
Unseen, the juddering coils and tubes,
Has faith in the all's-well electronic tolling
Of his father's astonishing heart, and lapses
Only once. An occasion.
Like that: dad's awake, asleep. The youth pockets
His not-very-old-man's poppy-field tract
With a zealot's unthinking; though, he's mortified
(Albeit silently)
By its clichéd passage into scrawled entropy:
Your old man will rise again and such and such, then
Under, dropping the pen. In shadowy opiate dreamlessness
Artificial as the room's sterility, blessedly, the elder
Cannot ponder the other's selfish whys and wherefores.
In it, the paradox that is the father's heaving chest
May continue puppeting life a moment.
In it, absence, sole respite of the stricken son in flight,
Cannot be sensed. Amen.

SURVIVOR, CUSTODIAN

In their profound spiritlessness, indefinitely,
Are bound by scionic obligation

This hollow of a house (Limbo) and

The tragically unbaptized soul;
That oldest of tales, narrated

Now by dissonant walnut and oak.

Gaping doors and voided shelves. It's forever
The final walk-through

To tabulate the rings, the errant branches left

Unlopped. No poltergeists, but—listen!
Termites ravaging the grain.

Their dust sifting from the beams a cruel,

Teeming testament to fact: even one day
The towering spruce.

THE RESTORATIVE POWER OF
TRAVELING *INBURRITO*

At sixteen, striking out, bravely, ambitiously, foolishly, on my own, it was disappointing to not be able to find foothold anywhere. My existence came to be a largely itinerant one, crashed on a friend's sofa, in bed for a week with my latest ill-matched romantic interest, or back for the briefest of stays at one of my parents' homes.

As a pierced, black-clad depressive in eyeliner, trying to make my way in the world, I was still a teenager, and therefore saddled with all the existential inquisitiveness and unslakable yearning for *something to do* inherent thereto. It's just that my options for fun were harder-won than those of run-of-the-mill bored Midwestern youth. I relied on the creativity and imagination of the handful of outsiders who could, on some level, relate.

Budding epicures and wannabe bohemians comprised my teenage quintet of quirky friends. Our idea of excitement was sneaking into wine tastings, crashing art school parties, and making scenes of ourselves in restaurants both hoity and toity. Like starveling rodents, we were drawn to anywhere offering free cheese. Countless decimated hors d'oeuvres tables were left in our wake; the staff of many fine establishments wrung their hands, terrified by the envisioned repercussions of asking us to leave, yet petrified by the scene we'd cause if left alone. Patrons, meanwhile, either looked on in discomfort or concentrated on ignoring our presence. We reveled on the fringe, unwanted by any culture but the microcosmic one we made for ourselves.

Then, around the time of my nineteenth birthday, that revelry ended. One friend murdered, another dead by his own hand; two months later, my father's death of a sudden illness. Whatever pathetic, sheltered notions of darkness I thought I'd known were revealed as so much navel-gazing. It was as if life wagged its finger at me, scolding, *You think you know what misery is, kid? Here, I'll show you misery.*

The death of my father forced me to grapple with the monumental loss of a beloved parent *and* the duty, as an only child, of tidying up what affairs he left behind. A harsh winter was encroaching when I moved into his house, my childhood home, to act as caretaker and executor of his estate. It wasn't the way in which I might have preferred to become a homeowner.

Part of what fell to me was the care of my father's purebred Pekingese lapdog, Gizmo. I slunk through vacant rooms, a haunted waif roaming aimlessly, picking up an item here or there, momentarily considering it, then setting it down again. Gizmo followed, nails *tick-tick*ing across the deeply polished hardwood floors. Even on my best days I simply wasn't much of a dog person. It was me, though, the only biped in our shared shelter from bitter winds and the ice that encased tree limbs and imprisoned the driveway, ensuring the two of us were well and truly stuck—it was me on whom Gizmo fixed his buggy eyes for guidance. But I was in no shape to give it. Under the circumstances, directing myself was challenge enough.

The brittle winter months I ordinarily loved for their peace and solitude were cold comfort as I picked through the accrual of stuff that was now all that remained of my father's adventuresome life. "Sell what you can, throw the rest out," had been the professional advice of the probate attorney I hired. He was adamant in his belief that an estate sale would be a waste of time. At first I had appreciated the lawyer's air of detachment. He was an indifferent man, all business. But how could he expect even as pragmatic a young man as me to decide the fate of the tchotchkes and random doodads scattered throughout that house, like the magical leavings of the Ephemera Fairy—let alone what was to become of Gizmo?

How to throw away the inexpertly painted watercolors, the hand-built latticework for orchids to grow on, or the shoeboxes of newspaper clippings? Even the bottle of flavored lubricant I excavated from an underwear drawer took on talismanic properties. (How much more heartbreakingly symbolic of one's humanity can a single item be?) The fireplace in front of which I often stationed myself, as a little boy, emitted ample warmth, yet in that house I still froze beyond any decisive movement.

My sole remaining friend, Brahm, encouraged me at every opportunity to get out and about. He was convinced that all I needed, in order to again become the Byron he knew and loved, was our signature brand of absurd frivolity. I doubted. Instead of listening to him, I resolved to let myself be drawn in, past the event horizon of the blackest of black holes. My resistance to feeling good was broadcast to the neighborhood by recurrent blasts of window-rattling German opera from the darkened house near the corner. If they thought me stranger for this, no one ever stopped by to say. Not that the neighbors had ever spoken to me before.

Brahm eventually infiltrated my hall of melancholy. One clear afternoon, he bought admittance with the currency he knew I would trade in, no matter how dour my mood (for I was and always have been a sucker for music): some new CDs.

"I brought some things," he said, triumphantly holding out a plastic sack full of aural pleasures. He hadn't called ahead. Though it was well after lunchtime, I still wore my robe, my hair a formless black mass, my face unshaven. Brahm easily pushed his tall, sturdy frame past me before I could tell him I wasn't in the mood for company. He said, "You've got a better stereo than me, so."

From anyone else it would signify an incomplete thought, but Brahm's "so" was always final, the concluding fanfare to a royal decree. It wasn't forceful, merely assured. I took a deep, resigned breath of the frigid air and shut the door behind him. Gizmo clicked along after the new arrival, seeming to sense Brahm's purposeful air. And why not? He wanted an alpha to follow. I made an atrocious one.

More than I wanted to admit, the throbbing electronic music my friend brought—uncharacteristically jaunty fare, considering his preference for dark metal bands with sanguinary names like Type O Negative and My Dying Bride—elevated my mood. As we listened, Brahm made a concession to my situation by helping me sort through a closet of my father's old clothes. Most I planned on donating to charity; though, some were worth trying to sell on eBay.

"Did he actually wear this stuff?" Brahm asked, grinning as he held up a gaudy paisley shirt.

"I don't think I ever saw him wear that, no." We were excavating a box, the contents of which hadn't seen light in nearly a decade. I pulled a short-sleeved aquamarine shirt with white buttons out of the mess, grimacing at its gaudiness. "This one either."

My friend chortled. "Wow, that's really awful. You should put it on."

"I'll wear this," I said, gamely pointing to the maroon abomination in his hands, "if you wear that."

Moments later we were in front of the full-length mirror on my father's bedroom door, laughing at how *normal* those secondhand shirts made us look.

"What I'm wondering," Brahm mused, "is whether these really are ridiculous or we're just used to dressing like we do."

"Wouldn't we know?"

We wouldn't. Nowhere in the four full drawers of my dresser, nor hanging from the rod in my closet, nor folded on my shelves, was so much as a stitch of color. Some ties on a rack and a couple of crisp white shirts for work were my only deviation from the black. Brahm's clothes weren't similarly monochromatic, but what colored garments he had were so outrageously unfashionable as to be an affront: bowling shoes with mismatched fluorescent laces, a hat made from a striped denim pant leg, a purple-and-yellow-and-brown plaid sport coat.

"We could find out," he said, tugging high shirt cuffs closer to the vicinity of his distant wrists. "Let's go get something to eat."

"In these?"

Encouraged by the fact that I was suddenly more concerned with sartorial matters than with maintaining my depression, Brahm was energized. He heaved down the big glass jug of pennies from atop my father's dresser. "Why not? You'll need to spend these someplace."

"Well, we might as well make the most of it, then, if we're dressing up." I handed him a pair of pleated khakis. "Here— these might fit you."

By the time we were outfitted, the two of us were in near-hysterics at our Casual Friday costumes. We'd never seen one another attired that way; it was beyond bizarre. I took all of the rings out of my ears. Brahm pulled his hair into a ponytail. For a finishing touch, we donned thick brown suede jackets from the hall closet.

"With our black hair, we look like super-pale Mexicans!" Brahm laughed, adding, "We're traveling *inburrito*—get it?"

The terrible pun stuck, as terrible puns should, and we continued snickering about it, uttering inanities in bad, half-remembered high-school Spanish, as we crossed town in Brahm's $400 Datsun, en route to a pizza place where we'd never be recognized. Except for a grocery excursion, it was my first time out of the house in weeks.

The streets and slick sidewalks were mostly devoid of traffic when we trudged into the pizzeria. My father's loafers pinched, distinctly unlike the Doc Martens boots I usually wore. A bell on the door tinkled at our entrance, and no one who turned at the sound let their gaze linger on us. Unheard of! Brahm and I ought to have been conspicuous, so fake, so baldly costumed—the patrons had to know what a sham our attire was! We seated ourselves. At any second I expected someone to leap up, pointing an accusatory finger, and demand, *What do you think this is, Halloween?* But the waitress came and went, paying as little attention to my algae-colored shirt as to the gallon of pennies next to me in the booth. We were passing!

For someone accustomed to blending in—that is, for one who was not shunned for so many years that he accepted his otherness as a mark of Cain, forever emblazoned upon his breast—the bizarre sensation my friend and I felt then cannot be adequately conveyed. *The Twilight Zone* makes a handy referent, however. This was the spy's first acceptance into a rival government's innermost circle. This was the transsexual's first great date in their role as the opposite gender. This was the light-skinned black man's first pre-integration sandwich at a whites-only luncheonette. This was, in other words, one memorable pizza buffet.

"You can pay me whenever you're ready," the waitress said with a smile, setting down our bill.

I wasn't even thinking about my father's creditors, his masterless little dog, or my grief. I smiled back, reaching to haul up the jug beside me. "Thanks, we're ready now."

The jug thudded on the wooden table. I expected our server to laugh and take in stride our plan to pay the entire balance of our lunch in copper coins (because, honestly, who does that?), but her expansive grin vanished in a blink, replaced by a Greek theater mask of ire. "You're not paying with those, are you?"

Brahm's sarcastic streak oozed out. "Well, it's US currency. You do take that here, right?"

"There's enough here to cover the bill," I chimed in, endeavoring to be helpful. "Plus a tip."

But she was having none of it. The waitress huffed off in search of her manager, who, when he arrived, turned out to be a heavy and disagreeable middle-aged man with a whistling nostril that cried out with skirling displeasure at having to listen to us make a case for inconveniencing his staff. His initial reaction, after we explained that the pennies were the only money we carried, was to threaten to call the cops. I called his bluff, reminding him that, small denomination or not, we had legal tender with which to pay. So the man changed tack and bargained, asking if one of us could maybe make an ATM run.

My wallet was at home; the contents of Brahm's were going to remain a mystery. A faux-Mexican standoff ensued.

The manager blinked first.

He lost, but defeat stole none of the man's bluster. Before taking his nasal acoustics to another part of the establishment, he tried one last grab for authority. "You guys are gonna sit here and count all that out, leave 'em in stacks of ten, and you"—he turned to the waitress—"are gonna watch 'em to make sure they don't try running outta here."

Thinking his rudeness had won us a measure of solidarity with the poor, embattled woman, I ventured, "Is he always such a jerk?"

The response I got was nothing but a steely glare. I commenced counting pennies.

Our bill and a gratuitous gratuity paid, the manager escorted Brahm and me to the exit. We'd eaten to contentedness and were fine letting him have the final word.

"Thanks for coming in," he said, too nicely to be genuine. "Now don't ever come back."

The little bell jingled as we stepped down, barely withholding our laughter, onto the grit- and salt-sprinkled sidewalk. As I glanced down to supervise my steps on that precarious surface, I was jolted again by the sight of the ill-fitting shoes, the canvas-colored pants, the godawful shirt.

A silent revelation: having donned clothing antithetical to my tastes, then appeared in a restaurant I'd never considered patronizing, I'd recovered a bit of myself—a little goofy, a tad daring, and, for the first time in months, kind of happy.

Brahm dropped me off at home, unable to resist making a last-minute admonition over the screeching hinges of his car door. "Hey, don't let traveling *inburrito* become a habit. I know you secretly like wearing this colorful shit."

They were good reasons, why I considered Brahm a friend.

Gizmo was waiting for me in the house, just inside the doorway, reeling with doggy joy at my return. I knelt to scratch behind his ear—perhaps our first moment of non-accidental physical contact.

"How are you, little buddy?" I asked, not even recognizing the endearment my father had used for his canine companion, coming from my own mouth. "Did you miss me?"

He threw back his otherworldly-looking head, dark eyes rolling wild, like a horse's, and answered me with a gargled, high-pitched *bow-wow*.

"Yeah," I said, stroking his silky coat, a tugging in my chest, "I missed me, too."

YEA VERILY, THE CHEESE
DIDST FLY

The closing of our favorite coffeehouse precipitated a panic
among its clientele. *Where do we hang out now?* we asked, des-
perate because we were young, therefore prone to lassitude,
and conscious of the legitimacy imparted upon time-wasting
by turning it into a group activity. The choice of which cof-
feehouse to frequent is not lightly nor easily made. As with a
favorite restaurant, club, or bar, it speaks volumes about a per-
son and is as individualized as taste in clothes. Unlike cloth-
ing, however, you can't just strip yourself of your coffeehouse
whenever the occasion suits—like a marriage, you're stuck
with it until one of you dies. (Or so my friends and I believed.)
It is, in other words, crucial for one to select wisely.

So the onetime patrons of "our" coffeehouse became a di-
aspora. Some migrated to the sleek new establishment down
the street—the one with the halogen lamps and brushed steel
accents. Others dispersed downtown, to that spot resembling
a sitcom set, with its overstuffed chairs and over-eclectic de-
cor. Still others resorted to the stuffy standby with the down-
stairs theater and that *Simpsons* pinball machine in the corner
that was beneath everyone to play. Starbucks was not part of
anyone's equation.

My friends Brahm and Paul found a lovably shabby place called Webstirs, a couple of blocks from where our former hangout now sat unoccupied. The personable owner was middle-aged, with a couple of inches' beard and John Lennon glasses. He explained to us that he'd bought the erstwhile church for the building's space, even after half the capital vanished with his runaway business partner. "We'd planned on it being an Internet café?" he said in his habitual way, with the interrogatory rising inflection that always made me think he was posing a riddle. "*Web*-stirs—get it?"

He served good enough java, but instead of a cybercafé he had ended up with a big space dotted with vacant sofas and a low stage serving no purpose. As if to prove to ourselves we hadn't picked the wrong coffeehouse (thereby admitting to a host of unspeakable character flaws), Brahm, Paul, and I were determined to help fill those sofa seats with patrons and make Webstirs a wild success. Maybe then its owner could actually invest in a few computers and stop having to explain his business's name to people. The three of us dipped into our own pockets to pay for promotional flyers, donated novelty mugs to the assortment decorating the coffeehouse's walls, and, in a singular moment of brilliance, thought up a weekly event to make use of that stage.

"Poetry open-mics are horrible," said Brahm from the sofa across from mine, his legs splayed out like he owned the place. At a minimum, Webstirs was like our foster child.

"Right," I said. "So we strip away the pretension, ramp up the irony. Why not? Everybody loves irony."

Paul broke in, always ready with a qualification. "Actually, a lot of people don't get irony. But people *would* like Bad Poetry Night, because it pokes fun at all the self-conscious crap you get at real poetry nights." He took a violent slurp of coffee that fogged the lenses of his thick-framed glasses. "Oh, and here's one: we'll let the audience throw cheese at people onstage! That'll break down some boundaries."

Paul loved keeping people in suspense. We waited impassively for an explanation as his eyeballs slowly defogged.

"Wadded-up balls of paper—yellow paper, only we call it cheese," he said at last. "Then it's interactive, not passive. Everybody gets some paper cheese when they walk in the door, and we encourage 'em to pelt the worst poet."

"Dude," said Brahm, impassioned by the premise. "At the end we could give the worst poet a prize."

"First place wins a jar of Vienna sausages," I said.

"Or a can of potted meat food product substitute stuff," said Brahm. We were on a roll.

"Some Always Save mackerel," Paul threw in.

"Man, you guys are great?" said the owner as he brought us all congratulatory free refills of the house blend.

For its inaugural evening, the turnout for Bad Poetry Night was surprising. People we'd never seen at Webstirs before appeared in the seats we'd rearranged opposite the stage. The flyers we had left in bookstores and tacked to the bulletin boards of rival coffeehouses had worked to draw a near-full house. Paul tottered around with a wicker basket, encouraging everyone to take from it their allotment of "cheese." As the only really sociable one of us, emcee duties fell to him by default. His big, dimply smile attested to how well he took to them.

"Hey, everybody, welcome to Webstirs and our first-ever Bad Poetry Night," he announced into the microphone. It sounded odd to hear his nasal voice amplified in a space I was accustomed to being quiet. "Our host"—he motioned to the owner at the counter—"and I will be doing the judging tonight, so I'm gonna recuse myself from performing, but let me get a show of hands and we'll put someone entertaining on this stage."

Paul called up a young brunette in a summer dress. After a hearty round of applause, she bravely recited a bad piece of free verse about a stray dog in a grocery store parking lot. A couple of balls of cheese arced up at the stage, probably hurled by the woman's friends. It was bad, sure, just not bad in a good way. No one laughed out loud.

Next was a girl with pink-and-blonde hair and a labret. She set the badness bar high, doing what looked like a half-improvised riff on the feminist free verse that sometimes got trotted out at other poetry free-for-alls: frequent invocation of her "sacred vagina," coupled with a burlesque of flailing arms and sneers. I thought she was hilarious, and assailed her with more than half my cheese, but a lot of the audience were too uncomfortable with the talk of lady-parts to react.

Paul called me to the stage next. Maybe it was because the first couple of performances had warmed them up, but I'd no sooner introduced myself—"My name is Byron, and the poem I'm reading tonight is about the best thing to write the worst poetry about: my ex-girlfriend"—than my vision filled with flying yellow balls. A couple of people groaned. The girl with the piercing threw all her cheese at me at once, then bent to pick pieces off the floor and throw those, too. From way in the back, Brahm heckled me, shouting, "You suck!"

"If you're through," I said, mock-smug, "I'd like to proceed. These twenty-four rhymed couplets are entitled 'Tears and Vomit.'"

More cheese, even more emphatic groans. It was great.

After my reading, just five more people went up to perform. One was a skinny kid in a backwards baseball cap. He was probably a couple of years younger than me, maybe seventeen. He took the stage meekly, shrinking from view into the bagginess of his black jeans, then mumbled into the mic, "'Sup, everybody. I'ma spit a little rhyme for y'all."

What followed was a five-minute rap full of pride and bluster and conviction that all but erased from memory the shy presence that had introduced it. Even unhip as I am, I could tell his rap was epic. He made growing up in white, middle-class suburbs sound like an actual struggle—grappling with identity, paying no mind to haters, arguing with Moms. Brahm's early scoff was put down quickly by Paul, who hissed, "So what if he doesn't get our idea of bad? At least he's got the balls to go up there and do his thing."

When the kid was done, he got a standing ovation while he slunk offstage, a wallflower once more. I was reminded of my first time performing for an audience—how liberating that had been, how shockingly rewarding to be so appreciated. The white Midwestern homeboy with the wallet chain had something in common with me. *How weird*, I thought.

"Okay, everybody, the judges have conferred," said Paul, mounting the stage one last time. "We'd like to thank you all for coming tonight, and the poets for sharing their, um, talent. We've decided to present the award for worst poem of the evening to Byron, who gave us that godawful rhyming verse about lost love. Byron, jeez, that was awful. Come up here and get your official Bad Poetry Night first-place ham loaf!"

The ham loaf had been an ideal prize choice. Its weight was almost enough to make me feel proud, holding it up and waving while twenty-odd strangers struck me appreciatively with balls of colored paper.

I wish I could say that our efforts with Bad Poetry Night were enough to save Webstirs from going out of business, like a fundraiser organized to save the beloved summer camp in some bawdy 1980s teen comedy. It would satisfy me to claim that the event reaped sufficient dividends for Webstirs to become the Internet café it was intended to be. Unfortunately, it didn't last the year. Our friendly hippie host closed shop overnight, without so much as returning the mugs we'd contributed. As divorcés, we swallowed our pride and moved on. Paul joined the downtown sitcom cast for awhile, slumped in one of many pastel armchairs for a season before coming to his senses. Brahm and I fell back in with prior acquaintances at a casual place near the university. Good coffee there; I liked the Sumatran. And the red-haired barista. If you're wondering about my ham loaf, it was re-awarded to a more deserving stranger at one of the final Bad Poetry Nights. I was unsentimental about it, and thus never learned if it was eventually eaten.

GRITS AS SALVATION FOR
THE SOCIAL LEPER

I am nineteen, the year being 1998, and my trim fingernails are lacquered blacker than the cheap coffee the waitress is pouring into my chipped mug. Brahm, my best (and arguably only) friend, sits catty-corner from me in the red-cushioned booth, his black hair swaying as he jauntily hums Barry Manilow's "Copacabana." His grin is irrepressible because he's just fed five dollars' worth of quarters to the jukebox—all of it to hear, rehear, re-rehear, et cetera, this same insipid song. Brahm prides himself on being the most tasteless person in the city, and I find this one of his most endearing traits. Beyond each other, predictably, neither of us has much of a social life.

"Don't you just love this song?" Brahm asks our young waitress. She smiles, oblivious to teetering on the precipice of a repetitive "Copa" hell. It's 1:00 A.M. and the earliest of the bar crowd have begun stumbling in. I wonder how she can smile when she's got to cope for eight hours with people like that.

As the song ends, restarts, and someone at a nearby table groans, my friend chortles into his fist.

I suppose that, if we have to be out in public, there are worse ways to entertain ourselves than by lounging in a check-

ered-floor diner. But my apartment is just across the street—
a historic former hotel in which I share a one-bedroom with
the most well-behaved cat on earth. It is impractical not to be
up there, wasting time in my living room, instead of paying
rent on this sparkly Formica six-top by swilling bottomless
mugs of acrid coffee. At my place there's a canister of dark-
roasted Guatamalan beside the grinder and coffeemaker.
At my place there are foodstuffs, bought and paid for: hot
cereal, quality sandwich components, as well as double-yolk
eggs and a small variety of cheeses for omelets. At my place
there are a good stereo and a few hundred albums, all within
convenient proximity to a comfortable sofa. Brahm neverthe-
less wants to be out and about, a monochromatic freak show
for fifty-odd diner patrons in varying states of intoxication.
So here we are.

If it weren't for my friend's cajoling, I might never leave home.
Give me the company of my cat and computer any day of the
week. After spending nearly two decades being exceptional
in one way or another—a painfully gifted child, a persecuted
tween, a dark and tragic teenager—I have just about given
up on people altogether. I am less embittered by them than
hopelessly confused. Disingenuous, illogical, spontaneous,
cruel—my opinion of humanity isn't a high one. The behav-
iors of my cat and computer I can at least anticipate.

In ten years I will learn that I have the autistic spectrum
disorder known as Asperger's syndrome. For now, though, I
am merely a geeky near-shut-in with a closetful of black, who
has a hard time wrapping his brain around why eating the
same hot cereal every morning, out of a specific bowl, using a
specific spoon, makes his friend laugh.

"Copa" is on something like its sixth play-through. I am about to suggest a departure when in walks our over-friendly mutual acquaintance, Joe. He's spotted us and approaching in his trademark fedora, lank and laconic and comfortable with, or oblivious to, his epic loserdom. Except something about his presence is amiss. It's an uncharacteristic showing by this passionless bore, and I for one am impressed: there are girls with him. Two of them. I barely notice the one clinging to Joe's arm, because the other is fair-skinned and willowy, with impossible-to-ignore red tresses to her waist. The trio sits. My misanthropy is no match for a pretty face.

Red has a pinup girl on her Zippo and a way of smoking her Parliament cigarettes that inspires me to remain for another round (or two) of joe. A pity, then, that my attraction doesn't cancel out an inability to initiate sane human conversation.

"Try the coffee," I blurt out, by way of hello. "It's diarrhea-licious."

Brahm half-chokes mid-sip, proving I am off to a terrific start.

Joe introduces everyone. The petite brunette adoringly attached to him is his new paramour, whose name I don't retain in my short-term memory, as I am good with names the way local car dealers are good commercial actors. Their lovely friend's is impossible to misplace: Molly. Remembering to employ etiquette, I accept her outstretched hand as if it's a baby bird, then give a minute nod. *Smile!* I shout at myself, inside my head. *Don't forget to make eye contact!*

Molly smirks around a sideways exhalation of smoke before announcing that she'll be ordering a hot cup of the diarrhea. My heart somersaults.

In typically unbidden fashion, Joe begins soliloquizing about a dream he had last night. Whoever famously said that there is nothing less interesting than listening to someone else describe their dreams must have known Joe. It isn't that he's intolerable, just a strong contender for Most Boring Man Alive. Dream monologues notwithstanding, what puts him in the running is his insistence that all guests to his apartment sit through the same French film about a melancholy middle-aged woman finding new love after the death of her husband. The film, as far as I know, never moves past her window boxes, from which the audience gets many maudlin shots of her mooning through the torrents of rain that sheet the glass. Both times Joe made me watch it, I fell asleep.

The way I stumble into romance is either by keeping my mouth shut and letting my "bad boy" appearance draw people in, or by speaking up and having my incidental, often inappropriate remarks mistaken for wit. My first girlfriends gravitated to what they perceived as my fringe-lurking mystery. They thought my crippling social phobia was sexy rebellion, like a goth James Dean. Too happy with that kind of attention, I didn't have the wherewithal to correct them. I was frightened of a lot of situations, back then. I still am.

At nineteen years old, I still haven't figured out how to converse naturally with objects of my attraction. A preponderance of lovely prospects get alarmed by my approaches. All too often I say the first things that come to mind—usually something decidedly unsexy, such as a reference to bowel distress.

But sometimes I get lucky. Sometimes, just sometimes, I meet a girl like Molly, who's all right with a bit of crass crossing her ruby-painted lips. There are also those flawless upward flourishes of her liquid eyeliner. Attention to detail, exceptional personal upkeep, remarkable physical beauty, and no qualms about poop jokes. Is it any wonder I am smitten?

The waitress reappears. I cannot tell whether or not she's exasperated by the population boom at our just-coffee-please booth. Joe stops talking and orders java. Ditto, his lady friend and Molly. The waitress sighs, perhaps unrelatedly. "Are you ready to order," she asks, as though caffeinated beverages were insufficient to constitute an order, "or do you need a couple minutes?"

"I'd like a few moments to peruse the menu," says Joe, faux-formal. It isn't his habit to carry more than five dollars on his person, so the request is a stall. The ladies second his intent, but only Molly actually extends an arm to retrieve a laminated menu card from atop the napkin dispenser.

Brahm catches me ogling her wrist's delicate freckles. He grins. "So, Molly, do you like Barry Manilow? Byron does. A lot. He's actually got this dance—"

"I don't, actually," I interrupt. In point of fact, though, I do have a unique dance; however, it's reserved for special occasions, Manilow songs not among them, when I am adequately stirred by the music and intoxicated beyond recalling the time it made my then-girlfriend cry. Brahm has seen it and wishes for everyone else to share the experience.

Molly's smile is wide. She asks, "Is it the Funky Chicken?"

"Oh, God," says Brahm. "It's so much worse. He's, like, the world's most awful dancer. His dance has special dark powers—hypnotic, really: you can't look away from it."

Joe interjects, "I had a dream a few nights ago that involved me dancing on a dark stage."

His girlfriend giggles. "Were you stripping?"

He's prevented from answering by the waitress's mercifully timed delivery of several coffees. With everyone thus embeveraged, she whips a pen and pad from her apron pocket, asking, "What can I get you folks tonight, then?"

Slothlike, Joe reaches belatedly for a menu and makes a halfhearted show of looking it over. "Nothing else for me and my sweet, thanks."

"I'm kind of hungry, but I don't want to pay for anything," muses Brahm. Earlier, he pooh-poohed my similar argument against corning here, denouncing it as an invalid excuse. Now he says, "I think I'll just stick with coffee."

"You guys suck," says Molly. "I'm not going to be the only one at this table eating, am I?" She turns to me. "Tell me you're eating something."

I love trying new restaurants. It's like a little adventure, going into an untried establishment, looking over all that they have on offer, and picking whatever looks best. The thing is, if my first experience there was good, I will order the same thing on every subsequent visit. It's as though the die is cast as I exit a restaurant's doors for the first time; nothing else can strike my fancy thereafter. The meal and the establishment are inexorably bound into one sensory experience from which I'm loath to deviate. For this reason, when I want a patty melt, the only place I will go is Nichol's Lunch, a greasy spoon that's been open since the 1920s. If I crave veal Parmigiana, I must visit Papagallo's, the overpriced Mafia hangout. When it's a savory platter of lamb *rogan josh* I cannot expunge from my mind, I go to India's Oven.

The first time I ate here, at this diner, was with my father, six years ago. His treat. I ate a Small Stack (three pancakes, wide as hubcaps), two scrambled eggs with cheese, and some bacon. My drink was coffee, which, although burned, was grown-up enough for my thirteen-year-old tastes. But the ownership has changed since then, as has the name on the neon in front. This diner looks identical in almost every way to the prior one; although, technically, it's not the same place. The menus are different. The staff, too. This continues to put me off balance every time I come, so I stick with the coffee and an occasional sampler platter of appetizers, despite the rubbery mozzarella sticks.

Tonight I'm hungry, but too broke for the sampler. I worry that it will disappoint Molly if I don't order *something*. Since disappointed girls don't give out phone numbers (not their own, anyway), there's additional pressure. I really, really want to get to know this girl. I want to get to know her as much as I do not want to order the menu's one edible item I have enough cash to order: a bowl of grits. Therefore, I do what any rational person would: I hedge.

"All that sounds good are grits," I say. "But I feel weird ordering the same thing I boil in eight minutes at home."

Molly's immaculate eyebrows go up. She asks, "You like grits?"

"Only with butter and sugar. I eat them every morning," I tell her, suspecting her question was the preamble to an accusation of unsophistication. I usually get those when someone learns how much I enjoy eating such simple gruel. Have I just blown my chances?

"Oh, my God, I *love* grits!" Molly says, like someone who's just won a sweepstakes. Her elegant hand is suddenly resting on my arm. I generally dislike being touched, but this is something different. She goes on. "Everybody thinks I'm such a freak. My roommate's always complaining about the kitchen smelling like wet corn."

I laugh when she does, only my laughter is born of relief.

"Wow," says Brahm, shaking his head at us. "You two ought to just order a big bowl of that crap and share it."

Molly, still with her marvelous smile, tells him, "That would be silly. He can come over to my place for a free bowl." She turns back to me. "Have you seen *Austin Powers?*"

"Who's he?" I ask.

"Yes, you are definitely coming home with me. Grits and a movie—good times!"

Molly and I drink a couple of refills of coffee, joking with one another and parrying Brahm's good-natured jibes. Joe tells another seemingly endless anecdote to no one in particular. His companion offers her thoughts on zombies and tells us how much fun she had playing one in a student film.

Hunger eventually gets the better of us, and that's when Molly asks if I'm ready for that bowl of grits.

The manager is maneuvering to unplug the jukebox, right as we walk out.

I ride to Molly's apartment. It's tidy. There's a nine-feet-wide oil painting of three female nudes—one of them with very long, very red hair—that draws my eyes before the fireplace and breakfast counter do. I barely have time to shed my coat before Molly takes charge of the situation. She's a blur in the kitchen: saucepans clattering, water running, dry corn product pouring. She tells me to make myself at home.

We eat sweet, buttery grits from blue ceramic bowls I don't mind, while, on her green sofa, watching a VHS copy of *Austin Powers: International Man of Mystery*. The movie is hilarious. She refuses to let me scrub the caked-on grits from her dishes when it's over.

"You can wash dishes next time, when we do this at your place," she says, then drives me home.

There is a next time. And another. And before I realize what's happening, I have a girlfriend. I may even like her more than the wet-corn smell of the food that brought us together.

DAWN

The blinds undrawn, the sunrise smearing on
the bedclothes, like butter on charred toast.

I make you tea you hardly drink, coffee for me.
Your lip is swollen, my abraded back complains;

we give in again to lust. How is it you're not aware
true love's not this bittersweet, nor tender?

A CASUAL PITCHFORKING

Being an oddball, it's only natural that I gravitate toward other eccentrics around whom dull moments are few and far between. Perhaps the most notable of my atypical associates were the Staff—Conrad, F.C., and Dave—all-American boys, by the looks of them, who nevertheless harbored three of the stranger souls I've had the rare privilege of knowing.

On the night in question, I stopped by Conrad and F.C.'s little rented house hoping only for banter and a bottle of beer. The gravel in their narrow driveway popped under my hulking Chrysler as I pulled in to find the usual shade-tree mechanic work afoot. "Diesel" Dave had driven his recently acquired vintage Lincoln over for a bit of maintenance. The pumpkin-orange behemoth loomed outside the garage, tilted up on a jack that didn't look substantial enough for the task. Dave languidly smoked a Marlboro in the driver's seat. From below, F.C.'s loose blue jeans and scuffed boots protruded. The scene looked like a dress rehearsal for a grease-monkey adaptation of *The Wizard of Oz*.

Besides the oil change and new three-dollar accelerator pump, my car, four years older than me, had cost less than $500. Conrad, F.C., Dave, and I all owned beaters purchased for around that price. We were all at an age when college should have been our focus, smart enough to have been bragging about our grades. Instead, being experts at assessing a rustbucket's value was our big point of pride. Many were the times that we followed up on classified ads that led us into tumbledown barns and cobwebbed garages, out in the sticks, to appraise a battered assemblage of big-block-powered Detroit steel. (And yes, we favored the luxury Chryslers. Their faded elegance spoke to us. Because we were barely in our twenties, we heard it, that clenched-jaw voice of privilege, demanding to be shown a good time. So we obliged, flooring gas pedals at every light, taking every corner like a hairpin turn, and generally treating our Mopar-era land yachts as two-ton toys.) To these cars we made modifications: bumpers fabricated from tube steel, expanded-plate window gratings, Krylon paint jobs, banks of completely pointless dashboard gauges. Passersby were forgiven their frequent allusions to *Mad Max*, but we couldn't stand people calling our vehicles anything so pretentious as "art cars."

I had barely been driving my still-stock '74 Chrysler Newport for a month. Thirty days was the minimum time the Staff and I accepted as necessary for a new car's personality to be understood. To make impatient mods was taboo, the pinnacle of amateurism. No idea of what the Newport wanted to be had gelled in my mind at that point; though, I knew it was just a matter of time.

"Greetings," said Conrad, through his shrunken, lopsided smile. He was still wearing a pastel dress shirt from his job at the antique rug shop, and was supervising F.C.'s work from afar, leaning against the corner of their enclosed backyard patio. I eyed the lager in his hand. Graciously, he noticed. "Beer's in the fridge."

My boots clomped up the wooden steps to their back door. In my ascent, I took note of the mason jars recently added to the assortment lined neatly on the porch shelves. I grabbed a bottle of Samuel Adams from the refrigerator and headed back outside. Sounding from somewhere deep in the house, just before I exited the kitchen, came a loud birdcall. The Staff did not keep birds. In fact, unless one counted the Nauga (a stuffed creature resembling a betoothed, wild-eyed owl), which the Staff kept bound in a strand of Christmas lights to contain its unspeakable evil, the only animal on the premises was Conrad's Burmese python, Carl, who was not given to musical outbursts. I tamped down my curiosity.

Hanging out with the Staff meant the only thing one could reasonably expect was the unexpected. And even the expected wouldn't necessarily be comprehensible. Both of them would deny the fact to their dying days, but F.C. and Conrad were Discordianists—adherents to a quasi-religious doctrine of chaos through subversive humor. The way I understood it, Discordianism arose in the late 1950s, after its founders experienced some wild stuff together under the influence of hallucinogenic drugs in a bowling alley. Me, I was just along for the ride.

"I see you made some more Jars," I remarked to Conrad, rejoining him in the backyard. Lighting a cigarette, I couldn't keep from asking, "Anything interesting?"

He shrugged. "One's Cinnamon Texas Pecan. The rest are Butternut Surprise."

"What's the Butternut Surprise made of?"

"Top secret. But its base is poop and buttermilk." He deadpanned, "You know, the usual."

Labeled with masking tape and Sharpie, Jars of Doom always bore pseudo-culinary names that belied their true nature as toxic bacterial playgrounds made of the most revolting ingredients imaginable, combined and left to "cure." A layman might say they were an ongoing experiment to manufacture unthinkable stink.

A three-week-old Jar containing, among other things, venison and muriatic acid once ate its way out of containment as we were reorganizing the porch shelves. The fetor that hissed forth actually made F.C. vomit into his gas mask. When I paid my next visit, days after the spill had been cleaned with industrial-purpose chemicals, I barely had the car door open before the Jar's mephitic tang—although tamer than before—overwhelmed me from the opposite side of the property.

There were other Jars of Doom that, upon disbursal, smelled worse. Those being traumatic memories, I choose not to recall them.

Below the Lincoln, F.C. banged and let fly a stream of curses. He emerged, after a moment, with a scowl and brandishing a wrench. His short dark hair was mussed crazily and his forearms bore scuffs of grime. "Hey," he called to me, momentarily forgetting his irritation. "Would you give me one of those smokes, man? I left mine inside."

Dave poked his head out of the Lincoln. "You all done down there?"

The wrench F.C. flung struck one of Dave's metal hubcaps with a reverberating *clang*.

"Will you give me a damn minute?" F.C. shouted. He took the cigarette I extended to him, then reached one grease-smeared hand into his pocket for *the Lighter*—a brass Zippo emblazoned with the Masonic pyramid-and-all-seeing-eye symbol. Unlike cigarettes, he always kept the Lighter within convenient reach.

"This piece of shit's giving me trouble," he said of the Lincoln. "I've been swearing at it for half an hour. Now it's time to smoke at it—that usually does the trick."

Conrad came over to ask, "How's the Newport treating you?"

The cooling engine ticked and pinged, a few paces behind me. I nodded approvingly. "It's running great, now that I've fixed the carb."

F.C. blew a petulant blast of smoke in Dave's direction, scratched his two-day stubble, and turned my way, brightening. "You see yet what I did to the Fairmont?"

The Fairmont was F.C.'s latest automotive acquisition, wedged alongside his other two cars in the drive: a compact 1980 Ford sedan he'd found for an unbeatable price. The elderly former owner had given it a thick coat of black house paint, brushstrokes plainly visible, before putting it on the market. For weeks after its purchase, F.C. had spoken about his desire to sand the body down to bare metal—a desire unfulfillable until the one-month waiting period expired. Asked what color he might paint it, he'd answered, "Rust. No paint, no primer—it'll just be Rust Car."

And so it was. He gave me a walk-around tour while Conrad stood at a distance, smirking. F.C. said, "It rained, like, the day after I stripped it. Kind of surprising how fast these streaks of rust developed. A couple days later, it looked just like this. Perfect oxidation, wouldn't you say? Anyway, it had enough character by then, welding the gun to the quarter panel seemed right."

The "gun" to which he referred was a perfectly aggressive appurtenance of postapocalyptic vehicle design. It was probably bits of a small transmission, but he'd refabricated it to look like a steampunk laser blaster, awesome in its ridiculousness.

Dave shouted for F.C. to finish the job he'd started. "You know," he hollered testily, "I've got someplace to be tonight."

F.C. ground his cigarette butt into the dirt with surprising calm before returning to work on our friend's brake lines. In a stage whisper, Conrad told me, "If he's not careful, F.C. might just cut them. It's a volunteer job, but Dave's been driving him like a rental car."

The reference wasn't lost on me as I took a bitter swig of my dark beer: it hadn't been two months earlier that the four of us had, rocketing down an abandoned road, launched a rented Saturn airborne. Our lives were one big rally race; rentals got the worst of it.

Dusk was settling when F.C. sent Dave, remarkably uninjured, on his way. The Lincoln let fly a spray of gravel before its tires squelched on the paved street: Diesel Dave's customary good-bye.

"So, what about you?" F.C. asked. He was wiping his hands with a filthy shop rag, eyeing my car. "When are you gonna let me do something to the Newport?"

"Like what?"

"Like weld something to it. You've been driving it for a month now, right?"

"That's really time enough, Byron," offered Conrad, like a counselor who's disappointed with his patient's lack of progress.

"Oh, man!" F.C. said. "I've got just the thing, too, in the garage. It'd be perfect."

Something in the way he stifled that boyish giggle made me leery. The last thing I wanted was an addition that would get me pulled over by police. Our modifications attracted cops' attention anyway, but the officers were usually more amused than concerned. Warily, I asked, "What is it?"

"No, no, you've got to let me do this. Trust me, it'll be great."

Torn, I weighed my options for a full five seconds before consenting to F.C.'s mystery mod with a deep, resigned sigh.

"Awesome!" he enthused, then practically skipped into the garage for his welding kit and the adornment with which I'd have to drive around indefinitely.

"Your new hood ornament!" he proclaimed, holding it up like a trophy he'd just won.

"Oh, come on," I tried to protest. "That's so stupid."

"I know," said my friend, grinning as he flicked the grinder on. Sparks flew.

The four-pronged head of a pitchfork was being welded to my hood.

A pitchfork. To my hood.

I groaned.

The smell of burning metal filled the air as the welder popped, throwing stark shadows over everything facing its bluish glare. It was such a simple job, over in seconds, and, when I turned my head back to see, there was suddenly a pointy, rusted farm implement jutting up from behind my blue leviathan's grill. As expected, it was absurd—a result at which my friends were pleased.

Much in the way a ship is christened before a maiden voyage by breaking a champagne bottle over her bow, the Staff commemorated inaugural modifications with layings on of foodstuffs.

When Conrad affixed a human-sized steel demon skull to the hood of his '67 Oldsmobile, the skull's railroad-spike horns were ornamented for weeks with a couple of large grapefruit. When F.C. installed a retractable rebar-and-canvas dorsal fin in the roof of his '86 Escort wagon, a salad was assembled on his hood, complete with croutons, ranch dressing, and place settings for four. When an air ram, made from a repurposed clothes-dryer vent hood, was bolted to my previous car—a '79 Pontiac—that vehicle got slathered in five gallons of yellow mustard that oozed its way into the vent system and made the interior smell like a delicatessen all winter.

Conrad produced a package of partially thawed chicken breasts from what seemed like thin air. (It would hardly have been a surprise to know he'd been carrying them on his person since my arrival.) His agile weaver's fingers tore into the cellophane wrapper and ripped free a single fillet. He raised his arm, then brought it down again in one smooth motion, making a kebab of the would-be dinner on the Newport's new appendage.

"They're not going to like this at work," I said with a grimace. "I'm going to have to park—"

Conrad silenced me by making a turkey noise.

"So much for all that," said F.C., standing back to admire his housemate's contribution. "Think I could get another smoke off you?"

We retired to their living room and the overstuffed comfort of F.C.'s tremendous brown sofa sectional. There, I learned the source of the earlier birdcall: a novelty wall clock that proclaimed the hours à la twelve different North American species—an enigma startlingly solved during a conversational lull at bluejay o'clock.

Following a couple hours' sitting around, I thanked them for the earlier beer and made for my car. All I could think about, as I turned the ignition key, was the coming weeks I was going to drive around, trapped with the smell of rancid fowl. If I were lucky, some wild animal would come steal it in the night. I'd remove the chicken breast myself, except such cheating was forbidden.

F.C. and Conrad stood, arms crossed, on the front porch as I backed out of their drive. Silhouetted against the Newport's headlight beams, the upthrust pitchfork looked preposterous. Even over the *glug-glug-glug* of the engine, I could hear my friends' cackling. As much as I hated the pitchfork and the many hassles I foresaw it bringing me, as I wheeled onto the pavement of that quiet street and watched the prongs bob with the motion of the car, I couldn't suppress my own smile. By the end of the block, the smile was a snicker. By the on-ramp to the highway home, the snicker was a belly laugh.

A pitchfork. And some chicken. In the course of my friendship with the Staff, this would hardly be the weirdest combination of objects I would encounter. If anything, they were some of the most normal—"normal" being wholly a matter of perspective.

CRASH

The tinkling aftermath of the upending:
coinage cascading from a region near my knees,
a silvery shower, and before these
concussed eyes spirals a hazy twinkling
galaxy where untold marvels of physics, chemistry,
and perhaps of life bear infinitesimal relation
to matters aerodynamic, tractive, inertial, or
relative to the structural cohesion
of subcompact sports coupes of Japanese
manufacture, here on Earth, when they double-ess
right off the road, into stone embankments, leaving
their youthful occupants fatally unwounded
despite their previous breakneck velocity. Then
the dark-gloved hand of driver sweeping glassy grit—oh.
He interrupts the show to ask,
"Are you alive?"

WORSE IS ALWAYS POSSIBLE

And we rise
Foolishly, impotent with ire
At what cannot
Not be:
The empty rooms, the silent hall,
The winter morning's doorknob shock,
The yawning of
The vacant bed beyond.
Selfish
Through it all, we are, to judge
By dint of three dimensions,
Immune to chance's promise of
A future. Somehow.
The electron's enviable
For its cloudy indifference,
But I, for one, can't imagine
An existence so small.

THE WAYS JUSTICE FAILS

They come for you when you're sleeping, bursting into your inner sanctum and surrounding your bed with their black presence. They paralyze you, first with terror, then with bonds of steel, and ferry you away to an inquisition where they work their every scheme to break you.

Or they come for you in the settling dusk of a long day, as you depart cheerfully from dinner with an old friend. They set upon you in the restaurant parking lot, forcing the flesh of your cheek into grit and coagulated motor oil. You cry out in alarm, involuntarily, but it only enhances the spectacle for passersby.

Or they do not come for you at all but bring you, instead, to them. An unexpected stop. *License and registration, please.* In a few moments, another car. Pistols in your face. Shouting. *You have the right to remain silent.* Your spouse in the car, frantic to know what's going on. *Anything you say can be used against you.* Everything recedes through the rear window— everything bathed in red and blue light—as the cruiser pulls away, toward uncertainty.

Either you know or you don't know. Whichever, they do not believe you. Even though it's the advice of everyone you've ever heard discuss the matter, your asking for a lawyer only invites suspicion. Your not asking for one lets them corral you into statements that will later be misconstrued. Later comes slowly.

Once they have you, even if only by a shirttail, the gears of the system, turning with punishing slowness, pull you further in, bit by bit, like a wood chipper the size of a courtroom. You will lose dear things: money, time, reputation. This is an inevitability. You will learn that guilt and innocence play small parts in this theater of strategy and social standing. How much justice are you able to afford?

The sleepless nights, the interminable days of jailhouse existence. You shake; though, it is not cold. Your lawyer, when you have occasion to see each other, seems concerned. Still, you wonder how much of that is merely professional courtesy. Is your innocence believed by this person entrusted with your life? Oh, but how could it not be, since you've only been truthful? Then again… (and again, and again, and again).

Everything is uncertain, and this makes you feel like you're clinging to a pendulum, swinging back and forth ad nauseam, and moving unmistakably in a third direction: down. You try to remain strong, resolute in the face of more opposition than you have ever known.

The trial. *He didn't cry*, the jurors say. Or, *He cried too much. Cold as ice* or *emotionally exaggerated.* Either way, you're sunk. The jury sees what it's told to, facts being immaterial when there are gut feelings at play.

So it's *guilty* even when it's not, and you're led out in shackles as some cry and others stoke the fires of their anger with the sight of you abased in chains. Inside, your own fire gutters. *How did this happen?* you think, as well as the opposite: *This can't be happening!* But it did and is, and there is nothing to be done about that now.

In prison you box yourself in to survive. A piece of yourself hidden away, safe, you become an automaton that performs its tasks because tasks are what it does. You downplay hope for fear of failure (hope not being hope until all grounds for hope are gone), but it's irrepressible and so still there as appeals go out and denials come in. Each time the courts deny you, you look ahead to next time, like a runner crashing through hurdles, failing but determined. You write brave letters full of bromides like, *Better luck next time; justice must prevail!*

You watch loved ones age. Some fall away. You wonder where the time has gone. You're a leaking hourglass, weeping dry time. It would be easier if you had a crime to regret committing.

When will it end? you wonder. When it ends.

MORNING NOSTALGIA

White. And there are only trucks down on the interstate as I look to the east, at the murky sun. Between there and here lies an improbable distance—maybe a third of a mile—hyphenated by a fence, electric, razor-wired, and aglitter with ice. Within the prison, the snow is clean and undisturbed, save four sets of footprints left by the bundled corrections officers during the nightly perimeter checks, and, if I angle my head sufficiently downward, the fence and the prints and even the walls of my cell fade into the periphery, and the drift beneath my narrow window becomes all I can see. Standing there like this, my cellmate silently breathing in his sleep a couple of feet away, I see the crystals at the crest of the drift one facet at a time, as each momentarily casts the morning rays. The perfect ridge is close. I could reach out and grasp a handful, I realize, were it not for this thick Lexan. It is prison's familiar torture: looking with mandatory detachment while never being permitted to touch.

I am all grown up and still envisioning snowball fights, sledding, those long, nose-chilling winter walks around town I used to cherish as much as almost anything. With my calf-length coat and the wool scarf without fringe my mother knitted me years into my adulthood, I would stay out for hours—a tiny, dark mote in a sea of white—walking nowhere in particular amid the muffled tranquility. There were sometimes partners with me on those hushed wanderings, whose intentions started out well enough, but whose hands inevitably numbed or teeth chattered, and one whose whole body often ached and shivered, so I'd enfold her in my coat and we would hasten back to the indoors, her saying over and over, "I hate the cold; I hate the cold," and me, oblivious, never recognizing the implications of that until the night she broke me over her knee like kindling.

I have long since forgiven her, but in these early moments of reflection, before the inexorable din of daily prison life crescendos, there is time enough for memories, however tender or sour, and to look eastward, past that fence and the field, the brown grove of trees and the busy highway, to the slowly ascending promise of day.

COLD

Ghosts of my fingers linger on the faux glass a moment, then fade. I smile at the chill. The temperature outside is low, but not yet hat-worthy. Good thing; I don't care for hats. Besides, after the week I've had, the wind on my scalp will soothe my overheated gray matter.

I have had cellmates criticize my weather-assessment method. With the Weather Channel just a couple of button-presses away, they think a glance outside and a touch of the cell's tall Lexan window is insufficient. Given the circumstances, it's silly to want to know the current dew point and three-day forecast. Few here own a truly warm coat. There are those, few and far between, who have been locked up since the days when you could order parkas and windbreakers and such. Even so, everyone settles for dressing in a sorry approximation of adequacy for the weather. A tactile check presents me with my binary options: hat/no hat, coat/no coat. It's not quantum mechanics. There aren't even scarves or earmuffs available to complicate the equation.

The charcoal fleece jacket I slide over my shoulders is mainly a symbolic thing—a gesture offering the illusion of choice. At least I can say its pockets are useful. In one I stow my CD player, in the other a couple of discs. My plan for this morning's chilly recreation period involves laying claim to one of the concrete picnic tables at the south end of the yard and watching hawks reel on their thermals for a couple of hours. If the sky offers no hawks, I can always turn my idle observations to the hunched shoulders of shivering loners as they rush along the boulevard. Someone is always en route to somewhere warm, indoors. Comical. As a person who enjoys temperatures below 50°, I am in a minority here, where they revel in the sweltering miasma of summer. The usual frenetic crowds will be absent today, my solitude guaranteed.

There's a piercing beep. From outside the cell comes the indistinct voice on the speaker calling, "Rec!" Everything announced over the speakers here sounds like the trombone-speak of adults on the *Peanuts* cartoons. It always has. Not even years of daily practice have helped me, nor anyone else, discern what is being said. Intuition and guesswork (and a little luck) lead me and five die-hard handball players toward the door. By the look of things, everyone else is sleeping late.

On the yard, I cross the grass and find the spot I'd been hoping for. I take my seat backward, elbows on the tabletop behind me. It's the sleepers' loss; the morning is a crisp and beautiful one. And with my music to drown out the distant hollow popping of a handball, it feels like it's all mine.

SIBERIAN EXILE

Observe: life aplenty, but nothing living
Nor beautiful. For beauty is unsatisfying,
Too fickle, too fleeting, and we speak
Only in absolutes, in *basso voce*, in taunts,
In outright lies; never may one permit his
Wrack-and-ruin teeth to chatter.

At one moment, in a certain light, might've
Been welcomed a little cold, a blast of ice for
These fevered souls, yet this tundra
—Arctic swath of bellicosity, sweeping
Northern winds, serpentine razor wire—threatens
To still so much love. But

It is more than temperature that carves
Out these scrimshaw bones, it is a chill
By which to shiver away while the gears that are
The tick-tock mechanism of senescence, of sons'
And daughters' narrowing faces, of wives'
Expanding emptiness grind inexhaustibly on.

PAR AVION

The card depicts Notre-Dame at dusk, in all its twelfth-century glory, rendered orange by the western sun. In the foreground runs the Seine. The haze of street lamps reflects from the bank. Their light is emerald on the water and dappled, making visible the subtle, intricate machinations of the current. I have stood on those ivied banks—right there, in the presence of antiquity—though it has been years, and the card's sender had no way of knowing this. She and I have never met, nor, indeed, exchanged any words at all. We are strangers in the truest sense, only now linked, however tenuously, by this simple token of kindness from one human being to another.

I receive these cards from all over the world—Australia, Texas, Germany, South Africa—signed with compassion, solidarity, or sympathy, and always with a little note to keep my head up, to stay strong, to remember the impermanence of all things. They never fail to bring me a sliver of happiness. It is too easy a thing, at times, to forget that kind people are out there—kind enough to write a few lines of encouragement to this pariah, without ulterior motives or expectations. The economies of time and funds make writing them all back impossible. Had I my way, each would receive a simple reply of thanks, detailing how important such things are to a man who has such limited scenery, so few warm words to enrich him and fuel the fires of his hope. To them (though they go on with their faraway lives and will never read this) I am immensely grateful, and forever hopeful that goodness, in its myriad guises, finds them at every opportunity. But for them, the gray that surrounds me would have been that tiny bit more pervasive.

THE THREE DISASTROUS
LOST LOVES OF B.

I once loved a sylph who mis-said *epitome*,
Garbled its little concluding *e*,
Rhymed it with *mobile home*. Dignity
Was given. I let the issue lie when she
Bragged, "I like my way better." Then we
Wrestled on the hard stairs messily.

I once loved a bivalve who lavished upon me
One year's bliss, then unexpectedly
Shut herself with a snap. Calls for three
Weeks on end all unanswered, until Denver: the
Irish pub, sodden fucking. Nary
A single pearly apology.

I once loved a siren whose cold voice could carry
Tragic lines to men out on the sea
Who came and came in futility
(For she was mine despite all of the contrary
Evidence). And when I finally
Saw, I fled, although am not yet free.

THE MIRACLE MATTRESS

It was like Christmas: I returned from a particularly tedious workday to discover that, in my absence from the cell, someone had not only remade my bed, they'd actually replaced it. A new mattress! What I'd left was an amorphous wafer of aging foam, covered in tan tarpaulin, but what I came back to was a spongy new slab, twice as thick as its predecessor. This sort of miracle ranks right up there with discovering an image of Jesus burnt into your French toast, or that elves have cobbled you a lovely new pair of shoes as you slept.

Mind you, in the twenty-two years before I was abducted by the state, I slept in a fair number of uncomfortable spots. Among them were train station platforms, classrooms, strangers' floors, and even—once—a parking garage. None of these, though, were long-term arrangements. None wreaked the chiropractic havoc I've known from my prison mattresses. Waking with a headache or pinched nerve from daring to sleep on my side is common, as is flopping around in the deep hours to find the sweet spot—a position that won't put my kneecaps to sleep.

My bed—*my* bed: the one I owned for three and a half years of serendipitous somnolence—was a king-size Serta. About it, one uncompensated reviewer declared, "The most comfort-able bed I've ever slept on." "*Soooo* comfy!" exclaimed another. And certainly there was room aplenty. I'm no *big* sleeper; I don't sprawl, as a rule. The freedom to loll, or lie crossways sometimes, on a whim, and occupy different space is never-theless a pleasurable thing. Plus, reclining with a good book, with my cats occupying their own regions of that pillow-topped plane—independent but proximal, like a pride in the African wilderness—was nice.

The downgrade to a heinously uncomfortable single was shocking. Compared to the other assorted travesties of my imprisonment, my sleeping accommodations are far from topping the list of the worst. This hasn't stopped me cursing with deep sincerity each of my 3,011 restless nights.

Of the 1,500 beds at Crossroads Correctional Center, my cellmate and I won the mattress lottery. Only fifty were delivered. I spied the difference immediately, and not just for my cellmate's valiant failure to restore the state of military crispness I fold and tuck my bedding into. The new mattress-es we few were issued dwarf the old ones. They're actually square-edged (no more shapeless lumpenness for me!) and lack those rips, holes, and burrs that sometimes worked their way through the sheet to poke me awake.

I wanted to jump up and down on it. Lacking that kind of headroom, however, I contented myself with hopping atop it. I did that stupid open-handed rub-and-push motion that people do in mattress showrooms the world over, and in those late-night mattress commercials. You know the ones. As if a good indicator of how well I'd sleep on it was how quickly it reformed after a gentle press! Under my weight, the sheets stretched loose of their tucks and receded, exposing the mat-tress's soft gray cover. To contend with the unexpected thickness, I realized, I'd have to make my bed differently now. A trade-off, then, but an eminently fair one.

The rest of the day, I walked around thinking of bedtime. I was like a kid who couldn't wait to get home from school and play with his new remote-controlled car. Maybe it wasn't exactly like Christmas. Close enough, though. Really close. And around here, I'll take what I can get.

LITERACY

Prison, it may surprise you to know, is no haven for the intelligentsia. When I was first cast so unceremoniously into a maximum-security institution (the tale behind which being a long, altogether unpleasant one), the culture shock was severe. I was a thin twenty-two-year-old, hardly a paragon of masculinity. Some would say I was an effete lad. It's certainly true that I was more at home with the pseudo-intellectual discussions at my local coffeehole than with the unchecked barbarism of the inner-city streets.

My first cellmate, "Roach," was from the country—*deep* in the country. He was also a lifetime underachiever, and prison was for him a second home. Surprisingly, he was sympathetic to my fish-out-of-water plight and offered his questionable advice on numerous aspects of my assimilation. Unless I bulked up quickly, he cautioned, it was inevitable that some "booty bandit" would swoop down and make me his "boy" (the modern, politically correct variant of "bitch"). Bald-headed and built like a plow horse, he invited me to join him and his Aryan buddies in their weightlifting. I needed very little persuading, being no fan of forcible butt sex.

There is safety in numbers, but that didn't make hanging out with Roach and his crowd any easier. Since I lack not only the Midwesterner's trademark twang but also the ability to use prison slang without sounding like an abject outsider, our vast gulf of differences yawned a little wider every time I opened my mouth. (I still refuse to employ the verb "holler at" in place of a respectable analog, like "talk to.") They got plenty of hearty guffaws out of my unfamiliarity with that standard country-boy accessory, the "coon-prick toothpick," and made no secret of begrudging my preference for quietly reading on my bunk over loitering with them for hours on the yard.

The fact was, they made me uncomfortable. I'd been raised by hippies in a happily nonsexist, nonracist, nonviolent granola home; I had no clue how to relate to Roach's pals, with their relentless bigotry and horseplay. A lost cause, it didn't take long for me to be dismissed as too book-smart for my own good. I won't say I was terrified at being abandoned in my threatening new environment, but Mum did always say that being different wouldn't be easy.

Somehow I managed to avoid becoming anyone's sex slave. After a couple of uncertain years, I even established a social network, of sorts, amid the population. It took no lifting of weights; though, I confess to cultivating some awful facial hair as a kind of camouflage against lurking butt pirates. In time, I grew confident enough to even shave it off.

The few individuals with whom I am friendly these days are mostly "old heads"—respected gray-hairs who have been incarcerated for long stretches of time. They have a general desire to stay well clear of the drama and danger so often incited by younger inmates. The old guys and I meet in the library, a couple of times a week, where we share travel stories, funny anecdotes, merciless snark about one another's respective age. (A common refrain from them: "You weren't even a glimmer in your father's eye, back then!"; a common one from me: "Sounds like someone didn't get his Geritol-Metamucil cocktail this morning.") We practically have our own reserved table. It's a comfort that there are others here with whom I can poke fun at the daily examples of ignorance and outright idiocy surrounding us.

Language is the air I breathe. Most of my time is spent in my cell, writing essays, stories, and letters while hunched over the typewriter. I'm sure I drive my cellmate out of his mind with this incessant *clack-clack-clack*ing, even though he's yet to complain.

As attuned as I am to matters of spelling, grammar, and usage, parsing the prison vernacular and noting the malaprops comes naturally. Now if only this skill did me more good.

All over the institution are these handwritten signs—hastily scrawled notes on white copier paper, bearing news that the gym is closed for the afternoon, that nurse's passes have been canceled, or that the canteen computers are down. They're often rife with unintended humor. In the visiting room, for example, inmates can have photos taken with their visitors, and these pictures are then printed, on the spot, on an inkjet printer. When the printer was on the fritz for a couple of months, however, and photos weren't turning out well, some anonymous staff member posted a warning sign to curb complaints:

PRINTER IS DISFUNCTIONING

Then there is this prominent notice, posted in the barber shop, amid cutesy, inspirational photocopies (surely you know the kind: the frog in the crane's beak, clutching its predator by the throat, above the caption "Never give up!!!" or the saccharine, big-eyed, tow-headed boy who proclaims he's special because "God don't make no junk!"):

BARBERS ONLY CAN USE EQUIPMENT

I couldn't say whether it's a warning to would-be self-stylists or an admonition against the barbers touching anything except the tools of their trade.

Predictably, the inmates fare no better. Not only did I once hear someone boast that he "didn't just fall off the tulip truck" (and thank goodness for that, since few things are worse than an injured Dutchman), an overheard conversation outside my cell door included an accusation that someone was "an obituary liar." One can only imagine what that's about.

A schizophrenic cellmate I once had for eight months (another story unto itself) loved solving the *USA Today* crossword puzzle. Then again, perhaps "solving" is a slight exaggeration. He enjoyed filling it in. After spending a few minutes to exhaust his abilities on ten or fifteen clues, he turned to me for help. Whether I had my nose in a book or was watching a rare bit of television was immaterial, as far as he was concerned; so long as blank squares remained on that grid, my immediate assistance was crucial.

He read off clues, one by one, telling me whatever letters he already had, and, #2 pencil poised eagerly over the page, waited for my reply. It didn't help matters that many of the answers he got on his own were wrong, thereby leaving me with a literary *Minesweeper* game, frequently uncertain as to how valid the hints he supplied me were.

Later on, long after our interminable cohabitation came to a merciful end, I saw him cutting hair in the barber shop. (That he was entrusted to "use equipment," including scissors, surely lent excitement to the otherwise ho-hum experience of getting a trim.) He lamented that his new cellmate was no help whatsoever with puzzle-solving. I didn't have the heart to suggest he try asking for assistance when the guy's favorite TV show *wasn't* on.

Selfish solicitation of my brain's surplus clock cycles happens often; although, it isn't always so intrusive. At times it's actually enjoyable. For aspiring romantics, I'm sometimes called upon to play Cyrano, helping them find that just-right way of proclaiming their limitless adoration of the girl they love, "without sounding, you know, all gay and shit." For the jailhouse attorneys, I'm often a proofreader of briefs. For a free-world writer friend, who mails me rough manuscripts every so often, as well as for incarcerated authors, I am a line editor. These are efforts I don't mind so much. At least they ensure my morning-to-night busyness, keeping me distracted as I await good news about my case—and that's priceless.

ONLY A FLEETING THING

Stepping outside after a visit, I am unprepared for the burst of icy wind that welcomes me back from several hours in another world. My breath actually catches. The shock of cold is one thing, but, as I round the wall of the visiting building, the scene of a sinking blood orange sun is in its own way breathtaking. It's a lurid panorama: puffs of distant vermilion clouds traced in blues and grays, and, higher, the streaked plumblacks of atmosphere. Space. But I cannot stop to provide the attention such a sunset sings for; my little trek is timed.

Past the lone guard tower I go, around the softball diamond, and up the walk to the housing unit, ugly and wide—the whole time leaning into the gusts, my ears stinging. From above comes a bubbling commotion that is a quavering line of eastward-listing geese. Just for an instant, but still so intensely that I feel it to the depths of me, I begrudge them the liberty of their wings.

PRISON BREAK

this time
i use
this time
for thinking
for writing
contraband
pen
in hand
smuggled in
and paper
for writing
folded twice
sustains me
this
contraband
pen
i hide
in my boot
from the guards
for writing
in fragments
at work
when not
working
sustains me
i use
this time

ANOTHER MAN'S BOXERS

The inaugural washing precedes the inaugural wearing, always. If the article must be dry-cleaned, then the inaugural wearing will have to be postponed even longer. I will wear nothing straight off the rack. There's no telling how many bodies have slithered through, nor how many hands have felt over a garment before my own. Washing also removes that intolerable starchiness, the telltale creases of articles that came in a package, and the whiff of plastic that all new clothing seems to carry.

Before the inaugural washing, there is a procedure to be followed—a preparation. Pockets must be checked for slips, collars for stays, folds for pins, hems for tags. I abhor labels, inside or out, and take great care to undo the stitching that affixes them, regardless of whether I bought the articles from a department store, a punk shop, or an upscale fashion boutique. My standards are uniform; I am very particular about my clothes. And yes, I recognize the apparent contradiction in paying $190 for a designer shirt, only to strip it of its fashion-house identification within moments of taking it out of the bag. It might even seem a tad rebellious—an act of protest against materialism, albeit a conflicted one, since I did buy the thing to wear—but all it is is an equal aversion to the scratchiness of clothing tags and the concept of becoming an uncompensated walking billboard.

Why buy designer clothes if I'm not interested in showing off a label's name? I choose clothing solely based on whether it meshes with my personal aesthetic, and if I could do that by shopping exclusively at, say, Old Navy, I'd be fine with that. Unfortunately for my bank account, the clothes that tend to fit my self-image best can be a little spendy. On the ultra-rare occasions when I flip through a men's magazine, like *GQ* or *Esquire*, my eye is only ever drawn to ads for military-inspired Burberry coats and the rock-and-roll schoolteacher look of the latest Belstaff line (yet indifferent to the presence of Ewan MacGregor therein). When I spot an item, in these magazines, that I fancy myself wearing, a glance at the retail price almost always sends me into sticker shock. It's my haute couture taste versus my notoriously thrifty ways. Then, of course, there's the further complications of black.

Waiting with a limo driver outside of a downtown Chicago bus depot, when I was twenty-two (a mildly amusing anecdote that will today go untold), I was asked, "So, are you in a band or something?" Calf-high Doc Martens, velvet trousers, a ribbed T-shirt, an ankle-length autumn coat—I suppose strangers could have been forgiven for mistaking one black-clad lad for the drum-machine programmer in some goth-industrial group. More often than I got the band question, though, I received disapproving looks. These generally failed to register. I only recognized the glaring physical difference between myself and Average Joe, ahead of me in line at the bakery, when he wouldn't stop turning around to check that I was maintaining a safe interpersonal distance. Piercings, eyeliner, and occasional black nail lacquer didn't help me blend into the crowd, either. So it was: I was a weir-do. At least I stayed true to myself.

I'd begun experimenting with my wardrobe palette shortly before my abduction by the state. Colors still tended to freak me out—wearing them felt somehow vulgar and false—but I had a handful of shirts in my closet that didn't: one in a mute red, one in bluish gray, one in deep burgundy. I was becoming very comfortable with charcoals. The ties I donned for work constituted my most garish peacocking. A week's worth of white Brooks Brothers button-downs hanging beside them were further proof of my assimilation efforts. Then, *pow*, all choice was taken away.

I spent more than a year wearing short-sleeved orange jumpsuits with *DETENTION CENTER* stenciled on the back, along with pinkish T-shirts, boxer shorts, and socks that, the previous week, had been worn by someone else. The tags in them could not be taken out, nor could the tang of cheap industrial laundry detergent. The scratchy collars and waistlines couldn't distract me from my fretting about what festering lesions or microscopic parasites the clothing's last wearer might pass along to me.

Then I arrived at prison. I was given a uniform—three of them, in fact, all in gray. It felt so good to be out of the jump-suit, with its eye-searing color, its lack of pockets in which to relax my worrying hands, its baggy midsection that I unnec-essarily grabbed to keep from sagging every time I stood up. The prison uniform's battleship gray was a relief, too. I knew some facilities issued uniforms in blue, some in white, some in green, some in tan. I knew also how much wearing any of these colors would depress me, as daily reminders of how far outside of my element I was being forced to live. Gray doesn't deserve its drab reputation; I was actually happy about this chromatic bit of compatibility. It almost made up for my continued deprivation from long sleeves.

Better still, the prison clothes were issued to me. They even had my name printed on the pockets, below my assigned DOC ID number. It would be my responsibility to keep them in good condition, to wash them, to not lose them. No one else had worn them, and no one else would. The clothing situation could have been so much worse. I was even allowed to remove the tags, first thing.

Years went by. Those uniforms have been replaced, piece by piece, many times since. There are schedules that dictate how long each article must be kept—boxers and socks, six months; T-shirts, a year; gray pants and shirts, three years—and I have mostly exchanged my old for new as those time frames allow. Financial cutbacks changed things. Staff who issue clothing here may now hand over an allotment of used T-shirts as likely as they might new ones. Ditto for gray pants, gray shirts, and underwear. Going to trade in my fraying, worn-thin items, I have thus far been lucky to get replacements that are still stiff from the box. I've hung on to a number of clothing articles for longer than most would. I have no desire to be given pre-worn boxers.

About the boxers, it's tempting to joke, "There are many pairs like them, but these are *mine*." Except they aren't mine. They belong to the state of Missouri, the same as gave me a number that I wear because the rules here demand it, but to which I lay no claim. I wear these cheap white boxer shorts because there's no alternative. If I'm ever handed a pair someone else has worn, I suppose I'll wear those, too, for the same reason. For now, I'm trying to make the pairs last that I've already got. There's no way for me to know if my next clothing exchange will yield more unworn stuff, or if my luck will hold. This strategy is a gamble, like a game of roulette. I hold tightly to the hope that I'll one day soon have the option back to bet on black.

SMOKE 'EM IF YOU GOT 'EM

What I'm about to describe to you is disgusting. As with many of the world's stomach-turning stories—the one about the boy and the sherbet container of frozen chicken fat, the one about the woman's devastating encounter with an airplane lavatory, the one about Orson Welles and the scandalized buffet-counter employee—the information I am about to share with you is also one-hundred-percent true.

You have heard about the value of tobacco products in prison. You may know, for example, that a pack of cigarettes is considered a fair trade for ten postage stamps or a shot of trash-bag hooch. You may also know that greater numbers of packs will buy even more impressive things: a cell with a better view, maybe someone named Peaches with whom to share that cell.

What might come as a surprise to you is that there are areas in prison where tobacco is prohibited. These are segregation units, where inmates are confined with even fewer privileges than normal, as a result of conduct violations. It's prison for the already imprisoned; residents call it the Hole. The prohibitive policies of the institutions do little to curb the tobacco trade in these places, frequent cell raids and strip searches be damned.

How? Well, this is where it gets unpleasant. I'm talking here about butt tobacco.

Packed tightly into numerous little balls, wrapped snug in the fingers of contraband plastic or latex gloves, then swallowed or, uh, *otherwise* introduced into one's innermost nooks, thousands of pounds of tobacco are muled, like so much marijuana through US border crossings, into segregation units of prisons across the country. [Source: Arbitrary Fake Statistic Generation Department.]

The idea of passing a bit of smokeable material through a stretch of one's digestive tract might offend some individuals' senses of what's fundamentally right or wrong. Smokers on the outside, particularly, will surely be revolted by the thought of this. Not that it makes it less offensive, but those little balloons are packaged with care, double- and triple-wrapped. It's in the best interests of those at both ends of the supply chain (so to speak). Not even the most addicted smoker wants to fire up a cigarette that reeks of untended nursing home.

Just the same, I know this happens all the time. In the Hole, desperate individuals will pay five dollars for just enough tobacco to fill up a standard-sized sugar packet, which is the going rate, and make it last a couple of days. Either they don't care or simply don't give consideration to the way it reached them. They just roll a pinch of it up in a page torn from their Bible's book of Revelation, light it with a double-A battery and some wire, and breathe deeply. And if, by some chance, there wafts up a whiff of campground outhouse as they take that first puff, there might be a moment's grumbling, but nobody asks for their money back. Refunds are probably a real pain in the ass.

THEATER OF SLEEP

I remember only being adrift in a roiling sea of mercury, un-der a sky like fresh-from-the-earth oil. My craft—a raft? a rowboat? a dinghy?—was thrown along, atop listless blobby waves. My eyes strained to the edges of sight, desperate for any trace of solidity. Maybe it lasted a few seconds, maybe a minute or two. It could have been an hour.

This haunting scene remained with me throughout the day, the way a song might have, affecting me anew as I sat at my desk at work, walked to the library that afternoon, and folded laundry before bed. My dreams have become, for better or for worse, nightly furloughs from the purgatory of prison existence. They typically make impressions that last. Like this one did.

Somewhere, probably in a book on neurobiology, I read that we cannot smell or taste in dreams, but that sensations of touch are common. This means it is either memory's notori-ous unreliability or a case of mind over matter that I once experienced a series of recurring dreams of such vividness and resonance that I actually started to wonder about the legitimacy of theories about reality's subjectivity. My waking life paled in comparison to the striking experiences of sleep, under which I lived out an intricate set of wanderings in exotic locales—along the banks of the wide, murky Amazon, atop dusty elephants in deepest India—and was surrounded at all times by a traveling troupe of outcast untouchables who loved me with a fervor and devotion unparalleled. We sang and danced along together, on our sojourn to nowhere, never speaking but reveling in one another's presence. I loved them all right back.

Every night, we languished in the heat of our surroundings, breathed the pungent breezes, and tasted the sticky heaviness of the air. Every morning was a return to unreality, the world paling in comparison to the lurid Technicolor of my wild places. The difference was that of the sweetness and delicate softness of the petals of a flower, contrasted against a shoddy painting of one. I grew concerned for my sanity as the dream world grew increasingly real-seeming, the real one more gauzy and eclipsed.

It continues to feel like a lived experience. Still I am able to consciously conjure the scenes of my verdant wildernesses, their smells of soil and distant fires. I recall these things with a level of precise recollection as keen as I have for places I have actually been, and there is no way for me to explain fully how this is. Lacking logical explanation, I've not spoken much about it. Friends who know me well enough understand why.

One quasi-spiritual, pseudo-transmigration aside, my dreams generally remain rooted in the realm of the banal. An oft-recurring theme has me walking the aisles of a market, selecting produce and eggs and such. Considering my affection for food and the process of shopping for it, this should hardly be surprising. I also adore the freedom of an open road, which renders equally obvious my repeated nighttime experience of driving a car down an inspiring stretch of interstate. Oftentimes I get to enjoy a fantastic evening in the company of friends. All of this without leaving my bed.

If dreams are a window to the unconscious mind, not merely a hodgepodge of fragments that are, as many neuroscientists believe, the byproduct of the brain's sorting and reorganizing itself, mine would reveal a deep attachment to mundane things—those whose absence is felt more as a persistent ache, like the broken bone of a limb too heavily relied on, than the stabbing agony of a stolen life considered in full.

DEEP-SIXING THE DOUBLE SIX
TO KEEP THE PEACE

There's a war on, a war seemingly without end. It is a war be-
tween the prisoners in our wing who play dominoes and the
prisoners who want some peace and quiet. It is a war fiercely
waged, and sometimes there are casualties.

The dominoes players have their regular table, where
they congregate for epic games of "bones." There they while
away the afternoons and evenings. Connoted by "epic" is
both that the games are lengthy and that they sound like
audio re-enactments of the Trojan and Peloponnesian wars,
complete with grunts, fearsome battle cries, and the clangor
of colliding shields. The players' enthusiasm for the game
is amply and often expressed. Not a day passes that they
neglect their precious pastime.

It's not an enthusiasm shared by everyone, of course, as
some of us wing residents are wet blankets and stodgy malcon-
tents with the zany notion that, outside of dire situations, one
shouldn't shout at another from anything less than a substantial
distance (and then, preferably, not indoors). We don't see much
point in getting wound up; it's only a game. Besides, some of us
are trying to use the phone… or hear ourselves think. The slam-
ming and the shouting—are they really called for?

Nonplayers address the players' racket in one of two ways: (1) they let the players' volume reach a level that can only be described as unconscionable before screaming an even louder "Hey!" and glaring pointedly; or (2) they steal one of the dominoes from the box when no one's looking. The first method only rarely has any effect. In this community populated with so many violent criminals, the passive-aggressive approach seems to be the more frequent one. Either way, the players never equate cause with effect. The sounds of battle always resume as soon as the set of dominoes is again made whole.

So, as I was seated on my usual perch at the far end of the upper tier, reading a collection of short works by Kafka and appreciating a rare mid-afternoon placidity, I wasn't surprised to learn someone had once more made off with one of the little ivory-colored tiles.

"Hey, excuse me," the lanky man—one of the players who'd journeyed far in his search, if he'd come all the way to me—said. "You seen the Big Six domino? You know where it went?"

"I wouldn't have any idea," I told him, making the eye contact crucial to avoiding his dangerous suspicion. Most of us who disapprove of the players' rudeness favor a policy of nonconfrontation, whereas they tend to go strongly in the opposite direction. I was in no mood just then to face off over someone's missing game piece. Even if I was, I wouldn't tell this person from a rival camp the fate of said trinket. "Someone probably threw it away," I said, adding hopefully, "or flushed it down their toilet."

My interlocutor scowled. I'm quiet and unobtrusive, yet also self-assured—a blank slate, a cypher, an X factor. He was sizing me up. Was I telling the truth, or did I know who'd sabotaged their fun? He finally shook his head, sufficiently convinced of my ignorance. "Man, some people!" he said, then turned away in resumption of his quest.

Maybe it will turn up, maybe it won't. My own selfish hopes lie on the latter. "Some people," indeed.

CON NAMES

The ruddy convict with prosthetics rocks
his trademark gait across the yard.
Legs rarely wears them,
his moniker mocking his lack, like
a one-eyed dog some smartass named Lucky.
When chauffeured around, chairbound,
by the toothless unshaven defective,
no one shouts, "What's up, Wheels?"
(Wouldn't want, after all, to be impolite.)
Others—Spider, Peanut Butter, Cheeseburger, Quick
(who wasn't quick enough), New York, L.A.,
hirsute Sugar, Justine, Peaches—
affirm what you've heard: clothes make the man.
Prison walls make no appearance in aphorism.
Who knows what mundanities of Mikedom,
Frankitude, or Joeness might
be buried in their previous lives. In
an occluded past, perhaps young Samuel
was all tough words and badness, not
wee little Sammy, penitentiary plaything. And there
but for the grace of God, some say.
Not I, foxhole atheist, who loathes any loss of will,
begrudging those with names once not their own.
I'll somehow, someday, leave this place and leave
no part of me, nor take. Nameless here forevermore.
An undignified death for so lofty a name,
he died years ago, but Caligula remains
a legend for his freedom with beatings

and endless boy toys, secretly envied by those who
eschew such entanglements—a rarity
for whom razor fences and locked-tight steel doors
unloosed vices-cum-virtues.

FADED FINERY AND
FRANKENFEET

When you first "come down"—that is, when you enter into
the custody of the Missouri Department of Corrections—
you're issued three pairs of elastic-waist gray pants, three
short-sleeved gray shirts, three white tees, four pairs of whit-
ish socks, five pairs of white boxers, a pair of black brogans, a
brown coat, and a fluorescent orange stocking cap. The pants
used to have fancy accoutrements like pockets and zipper
flies; the gray shirts used to button up and have handy breast
pockets; the hats used to be a muted blue. The issue used to
be larger, too, including additional clothes and a belt. If you
wanted more—anything colorful or warm or, I don't know,
hip—you had to mail order it through a catalog. Lots of in-
mates used to do so.

Then came Missouri Vocational Enterprises. MVE uses
prisoner labor, paid substantially below minimum wage, to
manufacture all kinds of important things for the Depart-
ment, from cleaning supplies and toilet paper to office furni-
ture and, yes, clothing. When the DOC awarded MVE the
contract to be the exclusive provider of clothing to its can-
teens, inmates were suddenly barred from ordering personal
hoodies, socks, jogging shorts, and so forth from any outside

vendor. The era of Dickies, Nike, and Hanes came to an end. MVE, with their cheap material and weak stitching, has since been the only show in town. Where its profits go is a closely guarded secret.

The old personal clothing was grandfathered, so no one's FUBU or Kansas City Chiefs gear got confiscated, but it has been many years since MVE got that lucrative contract. Not even well-made clothes hold together forever. So you see them all over the prison: tattered Jordan tees, once-red football jerseys gone high pink, puffy coats disgorging white tufts of fill at the elbows. The wearers are as proud of these rags as could be, even though some cling by only a few threads to their bodies. They strut around the yard, cocks of the walk, just pleased to be wearing something that isn't state-issued gray—a touch of individuality, even at the cost of looking like a hobo.

I arrived here before the MVE monopoly, and could have been one of the guys boasting a colorful wardrobe. I wasn't planning on being imprisoned long, though; getting comfortable was the last thing on my mind. Anyway, I *like* battleship gray. Then, in autumn of 2003, I broke down and ordered a charcoal-colored sweatshirt through the mail. Winters here get blustery. That sweatshirt was stolen a few months later, which I chose to regard as an object lesson in the ultimate pointlessness of acquisition (*Fight Club's* Tyler Durden would be proud). I did not replace it. I did, however, later buy an MVE fleece jacket that, at seventeen bucks, is hardly an extravagance. Everything else I wear is still state-issued—why spend money on more than what I need? Besides, the available clothing is nothing like what I wore before prison. Wearing tank tops or shorts now would make me less comfortable, not more.

But even I am guilty of going to the preservationist extremes my fellow prisoners employ, where certain items are concerned. One of my thick rubber shower shoes snapped off my foot mid-stride last week, en route back to my cell with a damp towel over my shoulder. I broke into a limp, sliding the broken left sandal along the walk as efficiently as I could, avoiding flesh-to-concrete contact like a practiced germophobe. Then there was a choice to be made. Either I could replace them with a pair of the flimsy new foam-and-rubber flip-flops sold now on the canteen, or I could sacrifice a perfectly serviceable needle and a length of thread from my sewing kit to stitch together my outmoded, cloven footwear.

The needle bent and blunted. I stabbed a finger bloodily. When the job was done, erratic black stitching zigzagged the shoe's top like the handiwork of a drunken frontier surgeon. But it held, so I've still got my shower shoes. I suppose such efforts are no different from someone else awkwardly patching a holey shirt he's had since 1994, even if that shirt's little more than a collar with a meager web of fiber that links tenuously to sleeves. We cling to what we can.

IN MEMORY OF MONUMENTS

The first to go was Otto's. I can remember precisely where I was standing and what I was doing when I got the news. Not that I'm some naive Pollyanna who thinks anything lasts forever—certainly not when it comes to restaurants—but I had a little investment in Otto's Malt Shop, emotionally speaking. My friends and I went there all the time, as much to soak up the airborne grease from the fryers as for the 1950s ambiance of the service-station-turned-diner.

I couldn't understand why the news took so long to reach me. It took a hookah bar to open in the same location before anyone deigned to mention the death of Otto's. No one wrote a conciliatory note: *Byron, I'm so sorry to have to tell you, but Otto's closed its doors for the last time yesterday. I know how much you liked it there. It's probably small comfort, but I promise to fix you a Ricky Ricardo when you get out, okay?* No one.

The last part may be just as well; my favorite menu item there wasn't the Ricky Ricardo, it was the Graceland—banana slices and chunky peanut butter on a half-pound hamburger. Sour grapes, though, right?

Nichol's Lunch went next. Unlike Otto's, which had been a relative newcomer to Kansas City's assortment of dives, Nichol's had been around since the '20s. There was a copy of their very first menu framed and hung on the north wall. A cup of coffee there used to cost three cents. Alongside the menu were decades' worth of newspaper pieces proclaiming the restaurant the "Best Place to Eat at 2:00 AM," the patty melts a tasty bargain.

It never mattered that the decor was tacky and dated twenty years ago, that the kitchen probably violated a litany of health codes, or that the tall redhead waitress had an Adam's apple and five o'clock shadow. Nichol's was where patrons from any walk of life could agree on something. The cheap fried food brought us all together, in a way. Nowhere else comes to mind at which conservative sexagenarians would peaceably sit at booths adjacent to those of drag queens *and* drunken frat members. It was a beautiful thing.

At least when Nichol's went out of business, the closing made every channel of the local news. Reverent elegies were delivered, in short on-scene clips, by many of the same fixtures I used to see on my many late nights there. Those brown tiles and nicotine-stained ceilings will be missed.

Very recently, a random craving for a gigantic reuben sandwich caused me to mention the New York Deli to my mother. The New York Deli was Kansas City's renowned home of the eight-dollar reuben. More than twenty-four inches around, piled high with a good three inches of pastrami and kraut, and almost impossible to eat without the aid of a utensil of some kind, there was no wondering why their reuben, specifically, was on my mind. "Oh, Sweetie," Mum lamented, "they closed. Last month, I think."

We used to go there every week when I was little. Their bakery supplied some of the best bagels I can remember eating. I vividly remember my excitement as a little boy at glimpsing their bright orange awnings. The sight was a sure sign a sweet, baked something would soon be mine to savor. When I grew up and went to live on my own, I continued going there, for onion, poppy seed, blueberry, or egg bagels. And for that huge reuben.

My disappointment was evident, sounding almost like desperation. "Seriously?" I pleaded. "Them too?"

Honestly, it isn't that Otto's Malt Shop, Nichol's Lunch, or the New York Deli were heartbreaking in their respective extinctions. I didn't know their owners, and generally wasn't more than passing acquaintances with the staff at any of these places. Besides that, big burgers and bagels, sizable sandwiches and specialty sodas can always be found elsewhere; another diner or deli will always open up, sometimes right around the corner from the old. What is substantially more difficult is accepting that I am becoming a foreigner, against my will and bit by bit, to a neighborhood I once called home. At the same time, in a certain sense, I never even left.

MY MOTHER, DYNAMO

The last Mother's Day we had together before my abduction, Mum and I brunched by the fountain at Roselle Court, at the Nelson-Atkins Museum of Art. Since I was a little boy, the museum has been a special place for both of us. On weekends we'd often come to see the exhibits and, during the week, there were wonderful art classes for children—pottery, figure drawing, and so on—that I was privileged enough to enjoy. Afterwards Mum would take me for a croissant or some other kind of treat in the softly lit neoclassical courtyard that opened off the museum's main hall. The place holds fond memories for us, as a result. Upon leaving that final time, I presented her with a large potted gardenia. It was in a full bloom of tiny white blossoms and was redolent of wild honey. Because of its size, she could not take it with her just then, so it endured the better part of a day riding around in the cavernous back seat of my old car. Eventually, though, it ended up in Mum's bedroom, where its delicate perfume could carry her into peaceful, pleasant dreams every night.

One month later, I was gone. During the nightmarish year to follow, she came to visit me twice a week in the county jail as I awaited trial. Often she would come with friends of mine who were there, I imagine, as much in support of her as of me. We all cleaved to one another—it was the only way to make it through. But mostly it was my mother whose face through that half-inch-thick safety glass both reassured and broke my sickened heart. For as long as I can remember, she has said that she's a survivor, and that time was my opportunity to witness firsthand the full reserves of her indomitable inner strength.

The gardenia I had given her, fragrant and soft with its hundreds of petals, soon shed and grew sparse with some unknown botanical illness. Strange white film had started forming on the leaves, like wax. Mum would deliver updates on its deteriorating condition: "I think it's dying." Not long after, it was moved to the glassed-in patio, where she would tend carefully to it, wiping each individual leaf clean. Even with that attention, the prognosis looked grim. It would have been nothing for her to abandon it to chance rather than dote on it the way she did.

Giving in is not generally part of her repertoire. The gardenia was finally able to be moved back indoors, able once again to cense her to sleep, in due course. She brought it back.

With me as well, her resolve has yet to flag, even these many years later. Still she makes the hour-long drive every week to see me, still we talk frequently on the phone, still she finds within herself energy enough to actively crusade for justice in the face of such obstacles as would drive most to discouragement. She is like a force of nature. From her own resilience I get so much of my own—not in some sociobiological sense of inheritance, but that I am emboldened by knowledge of her strength. And, for whatever it's worth, I wear for her my bravest face so she may take heart in the reciprocity of endurance.

We abide balanced upon one another's resolute love, and on the tenacious hope that, someday soon, I too will be brought back from my sorry condition, able on Mother's Days to honor her the way she so rightly deserves. And, of course, to give her flowers.

HIDDEN PICTURES OF
AN ELUSIVE PAST

After my abduction by the state, I granted indefinite use of
my computer to my mother, whose creaky desktop system
was generations out of date. It made sense that someone
should be using my PC, rather than let all those potential
clock cycles go to waste. I have always been bothered by
devices left to rust, so to speak, while there remains some
usefulness in them, and my workhorse of a computer was
no exception.

Mum isn't the tech-savviest person on the planet, so an
old friend made a DVD-ROM backup of my documents,
image files, and locally saved websites. (I had been an aspir-
ing professional web developer.) The last thing I wanted was
to be released from captivity only to discover precious data
wiped by some Trojan horse that had promised my credu-
lous mother virus protection. I was relieved by my friend's
foresight when my computer actually self-destructed a few
years later. The backup disc remained safely stored, and while
I never forgot about it, I did put it and its priceless contents
out of my mind for awhile.

You don't need to do time to understand how reflecting on past glories can preoccupy the man whose present is far from glorious, how the remembered self holds power over one who is locked up. I wear gray today, with white underclothes, but, like the visual representation retained by freed minds, in *The Matrix*, of their virtual selves, I too have a darkly clad residual self-image that favors tall boots—worlds removed from the prisoner in Chinese tennis shoes who does all he can to blend in. Just as the movie's character Neo is unsettled by the data port implanted in the back of his head, the feeling of my earlobes without the five rings I used to gently tug for comfort remains alien. Looking at my face in the scuffed metal mirror every morning, performing my pre-coffee ablutions, I know it isn't the true me gazing back, only an avatar, a construct designed by a system of repression. The real me is all in my head.

In escapist moments, when this system has the least control over my mind, I summon mental snapshots with all the specificity I can muster—of evenings spent cavorting goofily, of meaningful conversations, of past inspirational flashes, of sights seen in travels—and these happy entries from what Oscar Wilde termed "the diary that we all carry around with us" lift me out of purgatory for a while. But even having a better-than-average long-term memory, I lose the fidelity of long-ago events. Like ancient ink on parchment, many details are missing or illegible.

I came to suspect that indelible images, such as those preserved digitally, would serve me well as mnemonics for certain times I've let fall away.

"See if you can find that disc," I requested of my mother during a visit. I had been leafing through photographs that morning and was suddenly fixated on all those pictures sitting unviewed on the DVD-ROM my friend burned.

The blog on the personal site I maintained until 2001's interruption, was chockablock with pictures; I used to keep my digital camera at hand, because I never wanted to miss a photo op. I knew that my site had been preserved in its entirety, on disc, but couldn't remember offhand what candid shots awaited there, other than a couple from a trip to Chicago with friends, one of a fried-foods stand across from my apartment, and one of my cats sunning themselves on a light-streaked floor rug. Mum and I scheduled a time and date for her to talk me through the disc's contents, over the phone.

"I don't see that," she said, when I asked Mum to click on the Windows Explorer desktop icon.

"Okay, so do a search for it," I suggested.

She found the program, but what was in the window she described was nothing like what I expected. Where I'd wanted a straightforward directory tree that listed every file in a neat and sensible hierarchical structure, what was presented on Mum's screen was a menu of imprecise "user-friendly" options I didn't understand. I asked, "What the hell version of Windows are you running, anyway—Vista?"

Her response was silence.

We pressed bravely forward. I was reminded of why I used to be somewhat sought-after by acquaintances for tech support: I'm tenaciously unwilling to accept defeat, especially by a machine. "Try the name of my site, *Monochromatic*. It was also the name of the folder I had it saved to."

After a short delay, Mum spoke. "'No results found,' it says."

"Okay, then try the filename index.html. That's the splash page."

She sounded almost as dispirited as I was becoming. "No, Honey, it's not giving me anything."

For nearly another ten minutes, Mum played the role of my eyes, describing everything she saw onscreen, which

I upsampled into a mental screenshot and converted into instructions I tried to make comprehensible. I wanted to find those pictures so badly! Once we found out how to access them, getting her to print and snail-mail them to me would be no trouble at all. The disc they were on was *right there*. I would find them in seconds, on my own at the keyboard, even using an unfamiliar operating system, but our little game of high-tech blindman's bluff made me feel like a total Luddite.

Abruptly, then, a breakthrough. Mum said with a giggle, "Oh, wow, it's a slideshow!"

"What? What did you click?" I asked, desperate to know what she'd done. We wouldn't be able to repeat the results later if we didn't keep track of every action now.

"I don't know. There was an arrow," my mother answered. "Oh, here you are, playing the violin!"

"So you clicked a button with an arrow? Was there—"

"Now it's a photo of Anastasia."

"Okay, just wait a moment. Is there anyth—"

"Here's you in the back of a limo. I've never seen these."

She could have, of course. All of them used to be accessible to anyone who desired to keep up on the doings of one Mr. Byron Christopher Case. When I moved to Saint Louis, the year before my abduction, I redoubled my efforts at Internet visibility so friends back in Kansas City could at least be involved in my life vicariously. Some of them did, but Mum scarcely acknowledged e-mail's existence back then. These eleven-year-old pictures were all new to her, as evidenced by the enthusiasm with which she proceeded to narrate the slideshow: my friend Brahm on a telephone pole; my ex-fiancée, Bianca, hiding behind a graphic novel; my former roommate making an obscene hand gesture; my friends Mike and Chris cavorting on a seesaw; me posing absurdly on a park sculpture. It was too much.

"Mum," I said, "I'm going to let you go."

"What? Why?"

"I can't sit here and have you describe these pictures to me if I'm not going to be able to see them myself. It's depressing. I don't even remember some of the situations you're telling me about. It's like being taunted by the past."

We had come too tantalizingly close to the goal, and had spent so much phone time pursuing it, yet she understood. Always willing to visibly express emotion when I cannot, my empathetic mother's voice quavered on the other end of the line. "I'm sorry, Sweetie. I wish we didn't have to end like this today."

"It's all right," I said, in what I hoped was a reassuring tone. "Just pack the disc away again. I love you, and I'll see you Saturday."

I could have predicted that I would spend the rest of that day abiding one of my tension headaches. The weight pressing me down, following our photo-search debacle, wasn't too much to bear, though. I'm not generally one to dwell in states of ennui anymore; my depressive years are ancient history. It's true I began the day with an ill-fated phone call, which unfurled a host of frayed narratives in my mind, but it's also true that, in spite of that insidious headache, I donned my headphones, cued up a CD (one by a band formed recently enough to lack associations with preprison life), and threw myself into the preparation of some poems for submission to a literary journal. There is nothing quite like being in the flow of productivity, of being wholly in *the now*, to help me forget *the then* and the photographic evidence thereof.

DOING WITHOUT

It strikes me as odd. I couldn't hazard a guess as to what was the last meal to cross my lips, the topic of conversation with the last friend I saw, or the last piece of music to grace the soundtrack of my life as a free man, yet it requires no effort to vividly recall my last sexual contact with another human being.

We were engaged and sharing an apartment—one bedroom, one bath, two stories, two cats. She was twenty, I was twenty-two. Lovemaking was an everyday affair. Not in the sense that it was in any way boring, but that it was a constant. Because of regularity's tendency to benumb, there really oughtn't be any reason for our last time among so many to stand out in my mind as it does. But it does: her lifting the glass of Pinot Noir from my hand and whiskey-kissing me after dinner, the light smell of her short dark hair, our slender fingers interweaving as though they'd been meticulously crafted to lock just so....

Writing more about that night would be crass, but thinking about it is edifying, like regarding the stony ruins of a bygone civilization that strike dumb with their crumbled beauty. She and I lost touch years ago, tumbled apart at last, our past too overgrown with vines to clearly see anymore. Still, I carry my memory of that final melding together as I would a totem, held tight, a perfect moment in the life I once called mine.

Everyone deserves their allotment of sentimental dreaminess. This is a taste of my own. And that's all it is—sentimentality. Some call me "the Monk" for my spartan material needs, not for any aspiration to piety or chastity; however, I hardly obsess over the matters of the flesh. Over and over come people's questions about how I cope with this unnatural, enforced celibacy. Over and over I indulge the curious (as if it were any of their business) with answers. No, desperation hasn't found purchase. No, I've never been tempted by anyone around me here. At present, I have grander desires on which to focus. Carnality resides relatively low on my list of priorities.

It's there, though. Oh, it's there. Despite certain recurring allegations to the contrary, I *am* human, with all the accompanying physiological issues. And that damned sentimentality. More often than I'd prefer, I get stuck on the thought of how it would be, today, to clutch a certain someone close, share that intimate weight of bodies, sync two heartbeats, speak sharp-breathed solemnities, lift the scent from each other and slip with it into satiated dreams, to wake in the night, reach out, and be comforted by the warmth of a physical presence, by love. Then to rise in the morning and do it all again while the light slinks its way back toward the eastward windows. And to smile in the later day, happy for the lovely knowledge of another's naked secrets.

Of course, all this talk amounts to mere rambling by a man whose refuge now lies more within imagination than memory. After more than a decade, certitude means almost nothing; touch, so much more than I'll admit to even myself.

WHOSE KNEES

Whose knees are these
that ache and crackle when I stand to greet the morning
head count—a squinting face, glinting badge, through half-
inch Lexan glass—seven-forty on the dot? Thirty-some
years' use like sixty; a cartilaginous tear fifteen
calendars back. The prison doctor tut-tuts my twelve
spent treading concrete in inadequate footwear.
Too much strain, not enough exercise.
Indolence is my hobby. It's true,
I bind myself together now with words.
The cost of life: a writerly stoop,
once-perfect hands losing luster,
crepitus creeping on, and, of all things, it's this I choose
to bemoan, this daily grind of passed and passing time.

HUSH

The dining hall fills. Nearly 140 convicted men hurriedly eat the dinner they've been issued, then wait for the exit door to be opened. On any other evening there would scarcely be time to choke down half of what's on my tan plastic tray before guards rushed us out. Because we're about to be released to our recreation period, though, the fifteen-minute limit alotted by policy for each mealtime is not applied by the guards in charge. Staff enforce their rules selectively.

I clench my jaw and rub my thumb the way I do even when I'm not anxious. Earplugs aren't allowed here, and the noise of so many impatient souls in such a cavernous space is just shy of painful. The crowd's not usually this loud. It is turning into an evening replete with exceptions.

Twenty-five excruciating minutes crawl by. Twenty-six, twenty-seven, twenty-eight, twenty-nine. Then thirty. The basketballers are itching to play their game, the weightlifters are fidgeting in their seats, the library-bound are flipping idly through borrowed books. Conversations have grown even more emphatic. I'm about to put my fingers in my ears when there's a lull.

The lull lasts. *What?* Something is happening. I turn and scan for the sight that has calmed this madding crowd. *A brewing fight? Someone being taken to the Hole? The sighting of a woman whose appearance* wouldn't *sour milk?* No.

A downy tuft. One of those wispy, floating white globes of seed that are distributed on the wind—from what kind of tree or weed I'm too botanically ignorant to know. Someone must have kicked it up after it wafted through the door with us, over a half hour ago. Now it's suspended in midair, between tables, and nearly everyone is watching it drift. They're transfixed.

One lanky man with glasses blows at it and grins as the feathery little orb catches in his airstream. It sinks abruptly, then, and another man stretches out a tattooed hand to fan upward. Those within the tuft's proximity are united in unspoken urgency to keep it aloft. The scene is vaguely aquatic. Arms extend almost delicately from tables, like the undulating tentacles of octopuses, and smiles sprout with the suddenness of sea anemone blooms. The puff itself—langorous, incidental, aimless—reminds me of a jellyfish.

I'm not going to call this moment beautiful. Video of a discarded plastic grocery sack buffeted by breezes, performing air ballet, is a better exemplar of accidental profundity in that which has been discarded. I won't go there. Nor will I stretch to comment on the essential undercurrent of innocent joy in even society's most nefarious outcasts. (I'm not a *Chicken Soup for the Soul* kind of guy.) But in the full ninety seconds that that tiny seed holds the prisoners in delighted thrall, before it's forgotten and borne away by everyone's crushing move for the at-last-opened door, there's—I don't know—a kind of peace. And it's nice.

FIFTEEN LIFE LESSONS
PRISON HAS TAUGHT ME

1. Never share anything with anyone unless it's something you're prepared to lose.

2. Privacy, like joy, is a privilege, a precious resource.

3. Given sufficient hunger, even a taste for something like pickled beets can be acquired.

4. The criminally minded have a disproportionate statistical likelihood of really, *really* hating cats.

5. A disturbingly high number of men have a disturbingly low standard for personal hygiene.

6. Computer access is not, strictly speaking, required for survival.

7. Watching hometown news for glimpses of old stamping grounds is a sad, ineffectual way to preserve memories.

8. It is possible to make watercolors from the dyes in the shells of M&Ms candies, as well as to make paintbrushes from #2 pencils and your own hair, but the results are never satisfying.

9. That which you love most has the greatest potential to be your ruin.

10. Where half of everyone claims themselves "innocent," innocence is meaningless.

11. The line between boredom and depression is razor-blade thin; finding purpose can save your life *and* make it worth living.

12. How casually someone breaks their word is directly proportionate to the cruelty of their betrayal.

13. The goals of toilet training are not standardized, and not everyone's toilet training was devoid of subtle trauma.

14. It's an acceptable trade-off to spend several undignified moments being strip-searched every weekend, before and after a few hours spent visiting with good people.

15. Victimhood is a choice.

ACKNOWLEDGMENTS

Several people deserve thanks for the assorted roles they
filled in the six years this collection took to come together.
Most obvious is Jamie Jessop, without whose nudging to start
a blog I would have limited my prison dispatches to the realm
of ink on paper indefinitely. I also owe a debt of sincere grati-
tude to Sylvia McClellan, Sarah Locke, Kristin Summers,
and Lady Valarie Vogel, each of whom, by turns, selflessly
endured some obnoxious combination of analog-to-digital
tedium and my unblinking eye for misplaced punctuation.

My lifelong and, in truth, inexpressible thanks belong to
my parents, Dale and Evelyn Case, for their unique alchemi-
cal formula of DNA and TLC. I might never have turned
to writing if they had not indulged my creativity in so many
brilliant ways, encouraged me to question and observe relent-
lessly, and taught me that words, both written and read, make
for an admirable pastime. I never write anything without hav-
ing them somehow in mind.

COPYRIGHT NOTES

ABOUT THE AUTHOR

Byron Case is a writer and poet, wrongfully imprisoned since 2001, whose work appears in magazines and literary journals, as well as in the best-selling anthologies *Requiem for a Paper Bag* (Fireside, 2009) and *The Moment* (Harper Perennial, 2012). *The Pariah's Syntax* is his first book.

TO READ AN INTERVIEW WITH THE AUTHOR,
PLEASE VISIT REDBATBOOKS.COM